ATTENDING PARISHIONERS' SPIRITUAL GROWTH

THOMAS P. WILLIAMSEN

An Alban Institute Publication

Library of Congress Catalog Number 96-80118
ISBN 1-56699-179-X

DEDICATION

To my parents, who taught me to pray
To my wife, who constantly encourages me
To my children, who inspire me
To Christ Lutheran Church, Augustana Lutheran Church, and Gloria
    Dei! Lutheran Church, which offered me the opportunity to serve them

CONTENTS

ACKNOWLEDGMENTS

Thanks to JoAnn Friesner, who helped organize and type the manuscript, and to the Rev. Melissa Mahoney and Paul Stillwell for their encouragement and comments.

In 1952 my father took a parish in New York City. He was called to succeed Dr. Andreas Bersagel, a Norwegian-American legend, who was retiring. Dr. Bersagel invited Dad to attend his last confirmation class. One young confirmand came to class unprepared. The student complained, "I didn't have time to do my lesson because I had too much school work." Dr. Bersagel's Nordic eyes flamed as he replied, "Then you had better quit school!"

Whenever I tell that story, people either laugh or become upset. Both responses indicate that it seems absurd to think that spiritual training is more important than the "three Rs." Indeed, we live in a society that reveres science, technology, and medicine, yet undervalues the spiritual.

The Theme of the Book

The theme of this book is that *the primary purpose of the congregation is to assist and encourage people to grow deeper in their faith toward God, to become more lovingly intimate with God, and as a result to love God, others, and self more.* All the programs, ideas, and theological reflections discussed in this book address the issues involved in creating vital congregations that build up the laos for ministry in the world.

The church's gifts to the world are spiritually alive lay people empowered to live out their faith, active in love, where they dwell and work.

The better the church feeds; educates; fosters love for God, others, and self; and inspires their members for service, the more Christians will stimulate the world's people to serve one another. The task is daunting.

In the past forty years, parish ministry has changed dramatically and the role of the pastor has become more complicated. Parish clergy must master a great many skills and perform a growing list of tasks. We clergy are to be theologians, historians, congregational managers, directors of volunteer and paid staff, exegetes, counselors, preachers, teachers, and overseers of social ministry programs. In addition to those many roles, clergy need to be knowledgeable about contemporary social and political issues. Even this formidable list is incomplete. The dilemma I have seen in twenty-five years of ordained ministry in the Lutheran church is that with increased demands on clergy and congregations, the parishioner's spiritual and devotional life has either been taken for granted or relegated to a low priority. Then we wonder why the church lacks real spiritual depth and insight.

The Purpose of the Book

All ministry should be grounded on sound theology and scholarship, and rooted in biblical study and stimulating worship. The primary task of a congregation, however, is building up parishioners' intimate and experiential knowledge of God.

Martin Luther echoed the apostle Paul (Romans 10:17) when he maintained that faith comes through hearing. The pastoral and congregational tasks are to proclaim the Gospel and provide an environment in which spiritual growth can take place. This book discusses ways to make that environment possible.

This book provides an overview of a wide range of issues and programs, and a number of the chapters contain suggestions for further reading on specific topics. The book's ideas come from joyful and painful lessons of my own pastoral experience. I offer them with an abiding respect for parish ministry, in gratitude to The Alban Institute for making this book possible, and to Gloria Dei! Lutheran Church for giving me the time to write it.

The book is divided into four parts. Part 1 deals with the need for prayer and devotions. To be honest, churches in our day have done a poor job helping people develop a deep and intimate relationship with God. Chapter 1 speaks to that issue while chapters 2 and 3 briefly present ideas about Christian devotions and prayer.

Parts 2 and 3 are the heart of the book. Part 2 describes a ministry that can help people grow spiritually, while part 3 addresses the leadership required to carry out the ministry. The ministry and programs they describe are illustrative and given only as idea starters. Each congregation has to shape its ministry to fit its own personality and needs, but *something* needs to be done. Jacob Needleman, a Jewish author looking in on the Christian church, made an astute observation. He wrote, "The problem with Christianity [is its] inability to make itself known for what it really is."[1] Christians have lost the deep experiential understanding of what God's presence and the Christ-event mean. The church needs educated people of prayer to communicate this truth to a hungry world longing to hear it.

Part 4 describes the fruits of a life of prayer—for the church, the world, and individual Christians.

An old parable asks the question, If you have a seed for a tree that won't bear fruit until one hundred years after it is planted, what do you do? The answer is, Plant the seed. Our task is to plant seeds. God will help them grow in secret.

PART 1

Theological Reflections on the Theme

CHAPTER 1

The Need for Spiritual Nurture and the Experience of God

To prayer, we are indebted for penetrating those riches which are treasured up for us with our Heavenly Father. The necessity and utility of this exercise of prayer no words can sufficiently express.

—John Calvin

Cheese-Sandwich Spirituality

The following allegory illustrates the spiritual dilemma in the church. In the early 1900s, thousands of Norwegian families immigrated to the United States. They went primarily to Brooklyn, Chicago, the Dakotas, Minnesota, and Wisconsin. At the time, Norway had few job prospects for industrious young people. America held out great promise of fortune and security.

One young family, the Johnsons, dreamed of immigration. They were too poor, however, to afford the trip. Neighbors knew of their dreams and banded together, purchased passage in steerage, and gave them bread and cheese for the long journey.

The day for departure came. Mr. and Mrs. Johnson and their two children boarded the grand ocean liner for passage to New York. The Johnsons were from a small village and had never seen anything so wondrous as this ship, the *Stavanger*. They immediately went to the ship's steerage section, where they found a little corner to call their own. There they would stay until the ship reached port. They had enough cheese and bread to last the ten-day journey. The Johnsons were grateful for what they had and hopeful for what would come in America.

About six days into the trip, the son, Ole, said, "Dad, I can't look at one more cheese sandwich. I need something else to eat." The father, who was kind but very poor, took pity on Ole and sent him to the ship's store to buy an apple or other piece of fruit. Two hours went by. Ole never returned. Mr. Johnson became worried and set out to find his wayward son. Up flights of stairs he went. With each succeeding flight of stairs the surroundings grew more luxurious. Finally, after what seemed like hours, Mr. Johnson found Ole in the grand dining room. He was seated at a table surrounded by a banquet of food: fish, chicken, ham, potatoes, vegetables, fruit, and desserts.

The father's heart raced as he blurted out, "Son, what have you done? I can't pay for all this food. They'll put me in the brig."

"It's okay, Dad," interjected Ole as he gave his dad back the few silver coins. "The meal didn't cost anything. It's included in the price of the ticket. We could have been eating like this the whole trip."

Many people recognize their own spiritual poverty and embark on a journey they hope will lead to a deeper faith. Friends, family, and church members support and encourage them as best they can. The supporters offer provisions for the trek. Often the spiritual nourishment sustains a shallow spiritual existence, but it does not satisfy the travelers' deepest longings. It does not allow them to feast at the banquet table of our Lord. It is a cheese-sandwich spirituality. Consequently, many people "church-shop" or look outside the faith for more spiritually satisfying food. They become explorers, probing into the unknown reaches of the ship so they might be more intimately connected with God, discover meaning and purpose to their lives, and satisfy their hunger for some interior peace. They are on a quest for God, and they need guides who have feasted at God's abundant table of grace. The church has been called to shepherd these seekers on their spiritual voyages. Let us give them more than cheese sandwiches for the trip.

Facing My Own Spiritual Poverty

In June 1981 I moved to a new parish. To be more precise, I was called to develop a new congregation outside Annapolis, Maryland. I was not very excited about being a midwife at the birth of this congregational baby. After all, I was a successful pastor. I was ready for a large church, a prestigious church. The reward for my achievement was a church with zero members, an office in my home, and a sanctuary in an elementary school cafeteria with a ten-foot picture of a beaver on the wall. To put it simply, I did not want the job. In order for this new church to succeed, I needed an attitude change—and I was aware of it.

To this day I don't know why I accepted the call. I was angry, disappointed, frightened, and felt unprepared. I also knew I was spiritually impoverished. I could not, however, change my feelings. Fear and anger drove me to my knees. Prayer became my only weapon to fight the fear: fear of failure, fear of the unknown, and fear of knocking on all those doors. Prayer became my greatest resource for dealing with the anger— anger at myself for taking the job and anger at the ecclesiastical authorities for not giving me a more prestigious call. I was driven to my knees, not out of spiritual fervor but out of necessity. In the process, I was confronted by my own spiritual poverty. I realized that I did not have all the tools to grow a church on my own. My theological training had taught me that the Holy Spirit, not human initiative, grows churches. My task was to be spiritually prepared and faithful in my work, and then to offer my work to God. God would bless it and increase it. As a result, the next few years would become the most intensely prayerful time of my life.

God had been calling me to a deeper prayer life for years. I had resisted. God persisted and used this new call to drive me to prayer. Prayer is always the human response to divine initiative. At those times when we feel the need to pray, God has already begun the prayer within us. Because of my fear and anger, God knew that this congregation would succeed only if I was intimate with God. I remembered reading in Luther that normally he prayed three hours a day, except days when he was busy; then he prayed six hours. It seems an outlandish misuse of time to utilitarian people. Normally we think of prayer as a luxury for those with extra time. Luther turned that logic upside down. He maintained that prayer was the essential component of the busiest days. I found his insight to be true. If my work was to have meaning and purpose, it needed to be blessed by God, and I needed more spiritual sustenance than my "cheese-sandwich spirituality." I also needed help. I required a guide to direct me to God's banquet table of grace.

I knew I should see Father William of Holy Cross Abbey, a Cistercian monastery in Berryville, Virginia. Father William is a holy man. I call him "holy" not because he is a good man or a loving man, though he is. I call him holy because the presence of God is visible in his life. When I am with him, my thoughts turn to God. I come away from our discussions convinced that God has been in our midst. Father William, who has since moved, is a common man with an uncommon life of prayer and an uncommon love of God. He does not, however, have to speak of his prayer life or his love for God. One knows about those things simply by being in his presence. He inspired me to expand my prayer life and challenged me to preach what I practice and practice what I preach.

From June through October 1981, I knocked on 6,000 doors as a first step in developing this new congregation. Cold calling frightened me. I decided to make it a spiritual adventure and enfold this time in prayer. Each day before I began my calls, I spent at least thirty minutes in prayer. I would read scripture, pray for strength, wisdom, and love, and meditate on God's presence. As I walked from house to house I would thank God for the privilege of meeting one of God's children and pray that God would bless my next encounter. I remembered the painting of Jesus knocking on a door; it hung in my parent's home. Whenever I saw it, I thought of Jesus yearning to come into the house of my heart. During those five months of door knocking, it dawned on me that not only does Jesus knock on the door of our homes, but that when the door opens, Jesus answers it. Jesus, enfleshed in me, meets Jesus enfleshed in another. Thus, it becomes a holy encounter. Incarnation is God deep in the flesh of humankind. God is deep in my flesh and deep in your flesh. While on one level, I can comprehend the concept theologically, I can experience this holy encounter only as a result of being bathed in prayer. What this meant practically when I made cold calls was that my fear and anger disappeared like an April snow.

When I knocked on a door, Jesus answered it. I was neither frightened nor angry at Jesus. On the contrary, I was anxious to meet Jesus. The interesting thing is, some of those I visited also sensed this presence of Christ in our time together. I prayed not only before and during the visits, I prayed afterward as well. When I got home, I would pray for each person I visited. Then I would write him or her a little note. I also kept a list of people who seemed interested in the new church and would pray for them each and every day. It dawned on me one day that the focus of my life had changed. A successful career was no longer the most important thing in my life. Developing a new congregation did not even top the list. Meeting the Jesus in another person and praying for that person became life priorities. That feeling lasted until about September.

By September door knocking had become a tedious task. Simultaneously I grew weary of the spiritual discipline involved with cold calling. Instead of "meeting Jesus" in each person, my goal was to knock on as many doors as quickly as I could. I was the same, it seemed. By all outward appearances I was exuberant, dedicated, and excited about my work. No one, however, was interested in the church. They were cordial, and I felt the visits went well. They just did not care about a new congregation. I could not figure out what happened. "It must be the neighborhood," I reasoned. "If I change neighborhoods, maybe my luck will change." So I went to a whole new section. It didn't make any difference. Nobody cared. Finally, my wife reminded me that I was no longer praying before or after the visits. "A church does not grow because of charming people. A church grows because of the Holy Spirit working through faithful servants," she said. When I returned to my disciplined prayer life, the people changed. They were interested again. Obviously they did not change; I did. Or rather, God changed me.

Henri Nouwen said the first discipline we give up is the discipline of the heart—prayer. The church needs to confront its members with their own spiritual poverty, lead them into prayer, challenge them to have a disciplined devotional life, walk with them on their spiritual journeys, and pick them up when they fall.

Balancing Service and Nurture

Because clergy and congregational members have big hearts, they cannot sit idly by while others are in distress. This was especially evident in the 1960s, when many people's social consciousness was raised. The church became deeply committed to doing social ministry. Urban social programs were normative for city parishes. Congregations and pastors toiled in the cause of integration, did community organizing, started food pantries, delivered meals-on-wheels, ran programs for neighborhood children, and so forth.

The first ten years of my ministry were spent in the city of Baltimore. It was exciting and invigorating to be involved with so many outreach programs. Christians have served countless people. The church has made a difference. It did important work. A city council member remarked to me once, "I don't know what we [city government] would do if you in the church stopped your many programs. We could not afford to pick up the slack."

The work continues. Congregational members are busy participating on committees, both at church and in the community. Suburban, small town, and rural parishes also have become involved in service projects designed to aid their own members and minister to the community. Small group ministries have sprung up for singles, young couples, people who abuse drugs and alcohol, single parents, farmers, and others. It is good to see the church become more deeply involved in the human predicament.

The church, however, is struggling. Membership rolls have either dwindled or remained flat. Mainline denominations are in financial trouble. Ecclesiastical officials have become concerned about the viability of the institution of the church as a whole. Enter emphasis on evangelism and the church growth movement. "Grow and get more people involved in a small group" has become the battle cry. And we have tried. Greater numbers of people are serving on committees for Christian education, worship and music, property, social ministry, pastor-parish relations, personnel, long-range planning, fellowship, and the like than ever before.

All this is not a bad sign. The church needs to be a central part of the community and to serve God's people in a variety of meaningful and practical ways. Unfortunately, we have not succeeded as well in providing our people with the opportunity to grow deeper in their faith. Consequently, people burn out.

They grow weary because their cheese-sandwich spirituality has not provided the sustenance needed for service or given them the depth they seek in their lives. They are serving God without an experiential or *tasting* knowledge of God. The results have been harmful for the church and disastrous for religious people as a whole. People are looking for some meaning and purpose in their lives. But they are looking in all the wrong places. They expect success to give them a sense of satisfaction, materialism and wealth to afford security, technology to make life easier so there is more time for leisure, medicine to prolong life, psychology to provide self-understanding, sociology to confer self-worth, and science to help them understand their place in the universe. Indeed, those disciplines have helped us understand the world and our unique place in it.

They do not, however, ultimately satisfy. They do not convey wholeness. They do not bring us salvation. The great teaching of St. Paul is that there is no self-salvation. We cannot save ourselves by our works. Neither can we make ourselves whole by our knowledge or service. Wholeness and salvation are gifts from God.

While providing places to serve, the church needs to become more intentional about providing places for individuals to be nurtured and nourished spiritually. I tell my parishioners that they need to find one place to serve and one place to be nurtured. If they only have time for one, they should choose the nurture. The service will follow naturally.

The Challenge for the Church

The challenge for the church is to herald a vision of service that grows out of a person's deep spiritual connectedness to God and a sense of oneness with humankind. To achieve this kind of faith, active in love, it is mandatory for the church to be doctrinally sound, theologically contextual, liturgically vital, and spiritually active, invigorating, and refreshing. Cheese sandwiches will not do in a sophisticated world where hungry hearts cry out for greater nourishment and sustenance.

CHAPTER 2

The Art of Christian Devotions: Two Historical Models

Built into the deepest part of the human spirit is a desire for intimacy with God. The psalmist says it this way:

As a deer longs for flowing streams,
    so my soul longs for you, O God.
My soul thirsts for God,
    for the living God.
                    (Psalm 42:1-2)

This desire, longing, or thirsting for God is both similar to and different from desire for intimacy and community with other humans. God saw that "it is not good for the man to be alone" and made a companion for him (Genesis 2:18). This text not only illustrates the creation of family but communicates something much deeper. Humans have a natural inclination to be in community. Woven into the created fabric of humankind is the need to be in relationship with other people. Similarly, we humans long for a relationship with someone greater than our finite selves. In short, we long for God, the Creator.

While maintaining relationships with other humans is difficult, at least one can see, smell, touch, and speak to another person. God does not appear to be so easily accessible. Even if we are not proficient practitioners of the art of dialogue, we at least understand how human communication takes place. How does one communicate with God? Indeed, many ask an even more basic question: *Can* we communicate with God? Certainly God speaks to us through Scripture, sacraments, sermons, and the person of Jesus. God also speaks to us through prayer. Prayer is nothing more than dialogue with God. Just as most individuals need help fine-tuning their communications skills, so do people need help with prayer. Likewise, parishioners need models for daily devotions. What follows are two models for prayer, an ancient model and one that Martin Luther taught. I have found them to be helpful guides for teaching people about prayer.

An Ancient Monastic Model

In the early monastic movement, the monk's prayer life was described by four simple words: *lectio, meditatio, oratio,* and *contemplatio.*

Lectio or *lectio divina* (literally "divine" or "spiritual reading") refers to a recitation by memory of some sacred text. Because most ancient people were illiterate and owned few if any books, they committed large portions of the Bible and other spiritual writings to memory. During daily work, the monk would quietly recite over and over some meaningful text, usually from the psalms or the gospels. However, lectio divina is not just mindless recitation. Lectio includes being open to God's revelation. The monk understood that God communicated intimate truth about God's self through those recited texts. Lectio, then, was listening to the revealing word of God.

The early Christians' life revolved around lectio. They knew that the Word of God is not fully understood by simple reading or study. Lectio teaches the heart. As the words are recited, the words linger on the tongue and their beauty is savored. Lectio is slow repetition and can last anywhere from minutes to hours.

The Fathers of the church spoke of the Bible as a sacrament. It is a visible sign that holds the reality of salvation. It is given to the church so that we may listen to it. Lectio is the simplest form of a listening prayer. Dom Ambrose, of Bolton Abbey in Ireland, has been a monk for fifty years. He said, "The last thing I would give up in my spiritual life is lectio." It seems like a simple exercise that wastes precious time. In reality, it is the key that unlocks the heart and allows the saving word of God to enter.

Lectio divina reminds us that Scripture is more than a historical account of God's saving acts for humankind. It is more than retelling the two-thousand-year-old story of Jesus. It is a present encounter with the God who surrounds history. It is the recognition that the Word of God is always contemporary. That is why we relish each word as it is repeated and allow each word to find its way to the heart, the center of our being.

A natural result of this recitation is reflection upon the text, *meditatio.* Meditatio, or meditation, includes more than just thinking about the text. It is a prayerful interiorizing of the text's meaning so that it may be assimilated into one's life. For instance, the monk might meditate on the psalm verse: "As a deer longs for flowing streams, so my soul longs for you, O God" (Psalm 42:1).

Part of the meditation might include recollections of times when the monk was depressed or ill and God lifted him up. He might recall dry spiritual times when he drank from the water of life. In this context, the purpose of meditatio is to ask the questions, What is God saying to me through this text? and How does this text apply to my life?

The monk believed that as he recited the text, the words would pass from the lips into the mind for prayerful reflection, and then to its final destination, the heart. He knew God had the power to change the heart. A changed heart produces a loving, faith-filled response to God and others. This response to God takes the form of both action and speech. Action involves good deeds. Speech to God is called *oratio.* Oratio, or oral prayer, is the spontaneous response of the will to the text that was recited and reflected upon. This oral prayer may take the form of confession, petition, intercession, or simply thanksgiving and praise. Oratio is the oral response to the encounter with God's presence in the text.

Finally, there is *contemplatio,* or contemplation. When the one praying ran out of words and thoughts but the desire for God remained, the monk would simply rest in God's presence. In this resting or loving lingering with God, the mind and the heart began to experience this God whom they had been seeking. Contemplatio is the thirsty soul drinking the presence of God. What is experienced is a more intimate and loving knowledge of God. Allow me to illustrate by analogy.

When our children were toddlers, they would quite regularly ask my wife, Faye, or me to lie down with them while they went to sleep at night. One of us would lie with them for a while. First they would tell us about their day. They'd share exciting moments, sad moments, and relatively insignificant moments. After a while they would run out of things to say and would cuddle up close. No more words were spoken. They would simply close their eyes and rest in our arms. If we tried to leave before they were asleep, they would restrain us. At these moments our words weren't important—our presence was. Our presence communicated safety, warmth, and a feeling of belonging, among other things. Contemplatio is similar. Let me tell another story.

When our son, Erik, was five years old, we observed that he had not been feeling well and had been losing weight, so Faye took him to the doctor. With one quick test we knew the awful truth—Erik had juvenile diabetes. We rushed him to the hospital where Erik became acidotic and went into a coma. For days Faye and I took turns being with him in the pediatric intensive care unit. We held his hand and stroked his forehead. We said little. There was little to say. We lingered lovingly with him. He derived strength from our presence and from our being with him. Words were not only unnecessary, they were almost an encumbrance. Our presence spoke strength and hope more loudly than words ever could.

Prayer is similar. After a while we run out of things to share, things to ask for, concerns for others, and so on. We run out of words and we simply linger lovingly with the Lord and allow God to communicate with us in the silence of our minds and hearts. St. John of the Cross calls it "the prayer of loving attention." It is but a loving gaze upon our Lord who lingers near to us.

The early monks' prayer life had a natural rhythm. It began with the felt desire to drink of the water of life. It grew out of a desire not just to know more *about* God but to know God more intimately. The result was an experiential or tasting knowledge of God.

The Prayer Life of Martin Luther

It was Martin Luther's experience of God's grace through study of Scripture (lectio and meditatio) and prayer (oratio and contemplatio) that set in motion the movement that started the Reformation. Martin Luther not only reformed the content of doctrine but he restored to prayer a simplicity of form and intent—that of being with God.

The medieval devotional and penitential system was designed to have believers serve God and amend their lives without necessarily experiencing a tasting knowledge of God. Repentance and reform of life were ways of preparing the Christian for union with God. Luther reversed this. He declared quite clearly that the "inner person" must be trained by the Holy Spirit before the "outer person" can serve. Union with God is not the result of spiritual work but a gift given before any spiritual work is begun. For Luther, any movement in the relationship between God and humankind—even prayer—is initiated by God. Prayer is a God-initiated response to God. It is yielding to God and a constant attentiveness to God's working in us. The three powers of memory, intellect, and will do not reform the "inner person." It is God's working in us that changes us. Hear Luther in his own words:

> I believe that by my own understanding or strength I cannot believe in Jesus Christ my Lord or come to him, but the Holy Spirit has called me through the gospel, enlightened me with his gifts, made me holy, and kept me the in true faith,...[1]

Luther's theology of prayer begins with a statement of faith: Just as the actions of God bring me into salvation, so also does the action of God draw me into prayer, bring me into a relationship with God, and transform me from the inside out. Luther reversed the conventional thinking of his day. Medieval wisdom and practice grew out of an Aristotelian notion that those who do the good become the good—or that outer actions transform the inner person. Luther, on the other hand, was convinced by Paul's theology in Romans and Galatians that while we have some power over our exterior behavior, we have no power to change the "inner person." It is through the working of God *in* us that the inner person is transformed. This interior transformation effects a positive change in our outer actions. In other words, we are justified, made just, by grace through faith and not by good works. Luther's theology of prayer grows out of his theology of justification. Prayer offers to God the time and space for God to do the work of justification and sanctification in us. In that regard, prayer is more than our speaking to God. It is, in Luther's words, "standing silent before God and yielding ourselves to God so that God can work in us."

John Wesley's experience bears this out. We are changed from the inside out. In his journal we read the famous account of his conversion. "In the evening I went very unwillingly to a society in Aldersgate Street, where one was reading Luther's preface to the Romans. About a quarter before nine, as he was describing the change which God works in the heart through faith in Christ, I felt my heart strangely warmed." Three months later, on September 13, 1739, he wrote in his journal, "I believe new birth to be an inward thing; a change from inward wickedness to inward goodness; an entire change from our inmost nature...."2

Luther, like Wesley after him, not only spoke of the importance of prayer; he was himself a man of prayer. Luther left for the church a grand little book, written to his barber, describing his own method of prayer and entitled *A Simple Way to Pray*.3 In this book he translated his theology into practice and restored prayer to an ancient simplicity. Though Luther did not use the terms lectio, meditatio, oratio, and contemplatio, he incorporated each into his own personal prayer life.

Luther told his barber, Peter, that he should pray as soon as he wakened in the morning and as the last activity before sleep. As Luther instructed Peter, he also explained that he began his prayer time with lectio. And whenever he became cold or joyless, Luther went on, "I take my little psalter, hurry to my room,... I say quietly to myself, and word for word the Ten Commandments, the Creed, and, if I have time, some words of Christ or Paul or some Psalms, just as a little child might do." These are, he said, "God's words of comfort and instruction."4

Luther then reflected on each of the words recited, a kind of meditatio. He quoted from the psalms: "Blessed is he who meditates upon his law day and night" (Psalm 1:2). This recitation and reflection "warms the heart." Luther told Peter that when the heart had warmed, he should kneel or stand with folded hands and, with eyes toward heaven, begin to pray. The content of prayer is confession, thanksgiving, petition, and intercession. This is nothing other than oratio.

Luther's prayer did not end there, however, because he knew that contemplatio, or a prayer without words, was also part of the prayer time. Indeed, Luther often lost himself in such prayer. He "listened in silence" and tried not to obstruct the teaching of the Holy Spirit. He explained that, "the Holy Spirit himself preaches here, and one word of his sermon is far better than a thousand of our prayers."5

Finally, Luther reminded Master Peter that prayer is really an attitude of the heart and that the heart must be eager and ready to be in God's presence. He told Peter that as he concentrated his attention on the razor and hair when he was shaving or cutting, so must he more concentrate in the "singleness of his heart on God if it is to be a good prayer." John Doberstein translates "singleness of heart" as "prayer possessing the heart exclusively."6 His translation expresses clearly Luther's theology that all we have is gift. Faith is gift. Salvation is gift. Justification is gift. And prayer is gift that possesses us. The great reformer of Geneva, John Calvin, said, "Let the first rule of prayer be, to have our heart and mind framed as becomes those who are entering into converse with God."

This text from Luther is a great treasure and deserves to be widely read. All too often we stress Luther's doctrinal teaching without understanding the devotional practice that spawned it. This is not only dishonest, it is dangerous. It is dishonest because it was Luther's active spiritual life that informed and shaped his theology. It is dangerous because theology without spirituality degenerates into formalism, theological legalism, and rationalism. For Luther, prayer is the foundational act of the Christian's life. It is the root system that causes the tree to blossom. Remove the roots and the tree dies.

"Dear Master Peter," Luther wrote, "I give you the best I have; I tell you how I myself pray. May our Lord God grant you and everyone to do better! Amen."[7]

For Further Reading

Foster, Richard. *Prayer: Finding the Heart's True Home.* San Francisco: Harper Collins, 1992.

Keating, Abbot Thomas, OCSO; M. Basil Pennington; Thomas E. Clarke, S.J. *Finding Grace at the Center. Contemplative Prayer in the Christian Tradition: An Historical Perspective.* Still River, MA: St. Bede Publications, 1982, 35f.

Pennington, M. Basil. *Centering Prayer.* Garden City: New York Doubleday & Co. Inc, 1980.

CHAPTER 3

More about Devotions:
A Model Based on Ancient Truths

Eternal Father in Heaven,
I call to you from deep within.
Do not let me turn from you.
Hold me in your eternal truth
Until I reach my end.

—Annelein of Freiberg
from a hymn written shortly before the martyr-
dom of this Swiss Anabaptist

This chapter contains a practical illustration for using the ancient model
of the monks' rhythm of prayer and Luther's insights. It is about calling
to God "from deep within." The text we will use as the basis of the devotions is John 10:11: "I am the good shepherd. The good shepherd lays
down his life for the sheep."

Lectio

Begin by reciting the text six, ten, or twelve times so that you are familiar with every word. You might want to incorporate yourself and the
name of Jesus into the text. It would then read, "*Jesus* is the good shepherd. *Jesus* lays down his life for *me*." Repeat a portion of the text:
"Jesus is the good shepherd." Repeat it slowly. Emphasize different
words. "*Jesus* is the good shepherd." "Jesus is the *good* shepherd." "Jesus
is the good *shepherd*." Feel the different nuances of each recitation. Try
not to analyze. That will come later.

Repeat the second half of the text: "The good shepherd lays down his life for the sheep." Say it quietly and slowly a number of times. As above, emphasize different words. "The *good* shepherd lays down his life for the sheep," or "the good shepherd lays down his life for the *sheep*." Personalize the text: "The good shepherd lays down his life for *me*," or "*Jesus* lays down his life for *me*." Choose one of the variations that is most helpful. Repeat it slowly and silently for five to twenty minutes.

There are many variations on this one text alone. It is possible to use this text for the basis of devotions for a week or more. Each day's lectio could center around a different portion of the text. One word of caution: You might feel an inclination to begin reflecting on the text too soon. Try just to repeat the text or its variation without any reflection. Let the words flow through you. Allow the words to speak for themselves. Lectio is simply a time to bathe ourselves in the Word.

Meditatio

Meditatio is the time to reflect upon the text. Reflection can take many forms and be done on different levels. The form and level depend on the personality, spiritual maturity, and circumstances surrounding the one who is praying. It is important that this time of reflection does not lapse into an intellectualization about the text. Meditatio is not a time for exegetical study. It is a time to ask prayerfully, What is God saying to me in this text? or What message does this text have for my life? It is a time for personal reflection. It is a time for brutal honesty. For instance, we might reflect on times when we have felt alone and needed a good shepherd. We might remember God's hand lifting us up. Or we might recall times when we could not feel the presence of the good shepherd. It might be very appropriate to struggle with the hidden God, the hidden shepherd, or the "Deus Absconditus" Luther wrote about.

We might want to think of other shepherds in our life: parents, friends, mentors, and the like. We could also use this time to remind ourselves that shepherding is also our calling. We might want to reflect on the times when we shepherded others. Or we might remember opportunities when we failed to be good shepherds. Underneath all the reflection, we should be reminded of Jesus, the good shepherd who undergirds us in all times and in all places. One of the keys in this time of meditatio is to pay attention to recurring thoughts or feelings. They might be God directed. Sometimes it is necessary to abandon our own agenda. The best devotional times are often the moments when we become God directed. Indeed, sometimes we might abandon our prescribed text altogether or change texts in the middle of our devotions. As Luther says, "That's when the Holy Spirit speaks to us—so listen. One word from the Holy Spirit is better than a thousand words from our own lips."[1] Spend ten to twenty minutes meditating.

Oratio

While lectio and meditatio serve to bathe us in the Word, oratio is a time to empty the mind and heart of those things we need to share with God. Oratio may come at any time in the devotions. This model for devotions should not be so rigid that we short-circuit oral prayer. Indeed, we might feel the urge to pray any time during the course of the day. An honorable guideline is, whenever a prayer arises, pray it. God is probably calling us into prayer. It is, after all, God who initiates prayer. Whenever we feel the urge to pray, the prayer has already begun with the call of God.

This time of oral prayer can generally be divided into six kinds of prayer: confession, conversation, intercession, petition, thanksgiving, and praise. After immersion in the text, these prayers will come naturally.

Confession. Still using the good shepherd text as the basis for our devotions, we might confess those times when we did not want a shepherd. We might confess that we not only hid from the shepherd, but we hid from the flock or used the flock for our own purposes, and so on. We might not only confess our negligence to be sheep in God's flock, but our failure to shepherd those flocks we tend, for example, family, business, and the like.

Conversation. Quite often we just need to share with God our hopes, desires, disappointments, and even some of the trivial things that occur during the day. We can speak with God as we would any friend. This time of conversation might not seem to be important, but it is essential to deepening our friendship with God. This kind of prayer might be unrelated to the text or theme of the day. It is simply a time to share with God things that are on our mind.

Intercession. It is natural for us to think about certain people when we are in prayer. We all know people who need the good shepherd. We lay them before the good shepherd. We know that the good shepherd will lay down his life for them. What better place can we bring our loved ones than the arms of the good shepherd who leaves the ninety and nine and seeks out the one who is lost, alone, ill, or in despair? Indeed, we might even imagine the good shepherd carrying our loved ones in his arms.

Petition. If intercession is prayer for others, petition is prayer for ourselves. It is quite appropriate to pray for ourselves. We all need it. We all want it. We all yearn for the good shepherd's touch in our own life circumstances—illness, worry about work, parenting, or anything else. The good shepherd cares for each sheep—even me.

Thanksgiving. When we pray to the good shepherd, we can be confident that our prayers will be heard. We may also thank God for those times the good shepherd heard us in the past. It is natural to give thanks. This might be a good time to read a psalm of thanksgiving like Psalm 103: "Bless the LORD, O my soul, and all that is within me, bless God's holy name" (v. 1).

Praise. No time of prayer is complete without some time to give glory to God for God's love and mercy and the wonders of creation.

> Praise the Lord!
> Praise God in his sanctuary;
>   praise him in his mighty firmament!
> Praise him for his mighty deeds;
>   praise him according to his surpassing greatness!
> Praise him with trumpet sound;
>   praise him with lute and harp!
> Praise him with tambourine and dance;
>   praise him with strings and pipe!
> Praise him with clanging cymbals;
>   praise him with loud clashing cymbals!
> Let everything that breathes praise the Lord!
> Praise the Lord!
>   —Psalm 150

Contemplatio

Everything up to this point is preparation for contemplatio. Unfortunately, this major form of prayer is often neglected and sometimes maligned. It might be the deepest form of prayer. As mentioned previously, it is simply a resting in God or a loving lingering. It might also be called the prayer of adoration. In our context, it is simply a time for the sheep to snuggle up next to the shepherd. It is a time to gaze lovingly upon the good shepherd who neither slumbers nor sleeps. Let me illustrate with two examples. I own a golden retriever named Amber. She is always at my feet, always at my side. I don't know what she gets out of it, but she wants to be near me. So we need to be near God. In 1973, my wife, Faye, gave birth to our first child, Kaaren. As an infant, Kaaren slept much of the time. My wife would quite often get a chair, place it near the crib and just gaze upon Kaaren. It was a loving gaze. It was a gaze of adoration. Such is contemplatio.

We live in an age when people are seeking. They seek peace of mind, financial security, meaning and purpose, joy, hope, and the like. It is incumbent upon the church to direct people to the only one who can give us these gifts—God, the good shepherd. May God grant us the ability, desire, and the discipline to lead God's people.

Will people actually do this?

Ordinarily, people will not take the time to go from lectio through contemplatio. Generally one or two of the four forms of prayer will make sense or attract them. I usually teach the forms, however, all at one time. I have even used this model for the ninth-grade confirmation class. When I lead a group through a period of prayer using the four forms, I just vary the amount of time I allow for each form, depending on the group. (The ninth graders will last no more than fifteen minutes total.) I will lead the group through the exercise, giving examples of lectio, allowing time for meditation, moving through oral prayer, and ending with a time of silent attentiveness.

There are also wonderful teaching moments in parish life. When someone goes into surgery, I might simply suggest a form of lectio. I will have the person repeat for hours, "The Lord is my shepherd." I tell people this is no magical incantation but simply a way to focus on God's strength-giving presence.

Will people do this? Definitely—but in their own way and in their own time as desire and needs mandate and self-discipline allows.

PART 2

Fostering Spiritual Growth

CHAPTER 4

Adult Christian Education in the Congregation

Superficiality is the curse of our age. The desperate need today is not for a greater number of intelligent people, or gifted people, but for deep people.

—Richard Foster

Foundations

We humans have a natural inclination to investigate the world in which we live. Part of that native curiosity is the willingness to speculate about the beginning of the world and humankind's relationship to it. This inquisitiveness spawned science, philosophy, and theology. Theology examines God's interaction with the world. Theological investigation is both cognitive (intellectual) and experiential (mystical). All of us use both head and heart to some extent. Generally, we have a preference for one over the other. The way we probe into the divine mystery depends on our personality, gifts, and theological heritage. Nonetheless, it is essential to have a balanced approach in our search for God's presence in the world. We must balance the cognitive and the experiential, the mystical and the scholastic, the head and the heart. Our investigation requires all these and more. Let me illustrate with an analogy.

A professor of education gave his freshman college class an assignment: Learn everything you can about an orange. One group of students headed directly to the library. There they learned about the molecular structure of the orange; the amount of vitamin C in an orange; the best soil and climatic conditions in which to grow oranges; the average size, weight, and edible content of each orange; how thick the peel is; and various and sundry other things. Another band of researchers went to the supermarket. There they hustled to the produce section, purchased an orange, peeled it, and ate it. The first group knew everything *about* the orange, the second group *knew* the orange. Both, however, lacked some knowledge. Both failed the assignment. The orange does a person no good if it is not eaten. Neither can it be fully appreciated as a succulent citrus if it is not tasted. Likewise, without some knowledge about the orange, we would not know why it should be eaten, how many to eat, or how to grow them. Indeed, we might not even know that it is edible!

So it is with our relationship with God. Both the library of cognitive knowledge and the supermarket of experiential knowledge are essential to Christian maturity. For instance, the doctrine of confession and for-giveness is vital to the Christian witness. It has little meaning, however, to a guilt-encumbered person who does not feel forgiven.

Christian education tends to be unbalanced in both seminaries and in congregations. A congregational program of adult Christian education needs to include doctrine, biblical theology, mystical theology, ethics, and prayer.

Definitions

To be certain we are all on board the same train, a few definitions are in order.

Doctrine. Church historian Jaraslov Pelikan says, "Doctrine is what is believed, taught, and confessed."[1] Doctrine includes creed and conduct, theology and ethics. Doctrine is the business of the corporate structure of the church. It communicates what the church believes. The form of doc-trine is evidenced in devotions and liturgy. What is taught is the content of doctrine, namely, exegesis of Scripture communicated through pro-clamation. What is confessed is the testimony of the church articulated in creed and dogma.

Theology. Theology is scholarly reflection that focuses on specific doc-trinal themes. It is an ongoing process that endeavors to contextualize biblical truths and the doctrinal statements of the church.

Mystical Theology. This term is foreign to many protestants. Jurgen
Moltmann declares that its aim is a spiritual wisdom drawn more from
experience than from doctrine. The theology itself is not mystical. It is
mystical only because through it, people try to express in words the experience of God. It is impossible, however, to convey accurately and
completely a human experience. Consequently, the language of mystical
theology is metaphor and analogy and addresses primarily the journey or
the voyage to the experience but not the experience itself. Its purpose is
to elucidate the personal realization of the doctrine of the church. Its
result is to convey a new and deeper understanding of God. A Cistercian
monk told me that St. Bernard would quite regularly tell his brothers,
"Today we shall read from the theological book of experience." Mystical
theology is nothing more than the record of individual human experience
of God.

Spirituality. Because this is a book about developing a deep spirituality
in congregational members, it is important to describe what a vibrant and
mature spirituality is. Christian spirituality has as its starting point the
Incarnation and Pentecost. It begins with the understanding that God is
deep in the flesh of humankind. To say that we are spiritual is to suggest
that our spirits are capable of receiving the indwelling spirit of God.

Spirituality is a continual attentiveness to God's self-disclosure
through prayer, worship, and study. It is discovering ways we can love
God through service to humankind. Through the attentiveness of spirituality, a person's life is made vibrant, vigorous, and compassionate. It is a
holy life created by God.

Spirituality is a process of transformation. It is growth in holiness. It
is evidenced by an ever-deepening love of God, self, and neighbor. It is
the metamorphosis of the whole person—head, heart, and will. St. Paul
describes it as a transformation of the *mind* whereby the mind becomes
capable of discerning God's *will* (Romans 12:2). He reminds us that it is
a continuing creation of a new *heart*: "God's love has been poured into
our hearts through the Holy Spirit that has been given to us" (5:5). He
proclaims in bold letters that the spiritual person is a "new creation"
(Galatians 6:15). He holds out the promise of a new life in which our old
ways die and Christ is formed and lives in us (2:20 and 4:19). And he
declares it to be a holy life that "lives by the spirit" and is "guided by the
spirit" (5:25).

At its best, spirituality combines the cognitive and the experiential, the scholastic and the mystical. We cannot divorce the head from the heart, feelings from thinking, or the intellect from personal experience.

Finally, mature Christian spirituality describes a state in which the three traditional functions of humankind—the intellect, the affections, and the will—are in concord with the intellect, the affections, and the will of God. The Eastern Church calls this state divinization. The West calls it sanctification. It is nothing less than a person being recreated in the image and likeness of God.

The educational programs of the congregation should be so designed that the head is challenged and trained, the heart is transformed by the experience of the indwelling spirit, and the will generates a life of love.

CHAPTER 5

Adult Spiritual Education: A Revised Paradigm

The teaching ministry of the congregation is vital to the health and well-being of individual members and the congregation as a whole. Local churches have a unique opportunity to touch people in their deepest interior places. Most Christians, however, end their formal religious and spiritual education at confirmation. Consequently their growth is stunted and their faith shallow. Intentional and well-planned adult education grounds people in biblical theology and the historical doctrinal truths of the church. It provides space, time, and opportunity for God to work in their hearts. It encourages them to take their faith seriously in their ethical decision making. It trains leaders, challenges parishioners to think spiritually and theologically, and helps shape their worldview. It instructs the head and touches the heart. The congregation can be a university in miniature that offers a variety of educational opportunities not available anywhere else.

Training the Mind

Sunday Morning Adult Education

Sunday morning is the best time to get adults involved in education. In the parish I serve, Gloria Dei! Lutheran Church, about one-fourth of the worshipping adults regularly attend Sunday school. Seventy-five percent of the time, one of the pastors teaches the class. It is important for the pastor to teach on Sunday morning. The pastor is not only theologically

trained, she is the one charged with the primary responsibility for parishioners' souls. I realize adult forums are popular, but they can take place
during the week. Sunday should be a time to teach the doctrines of the
church, work through exegetically sound Bible studies, discuss Christian
ethics, and guide people in prayer. I know this creates an added burden
for the pastor on Sunday morning, especially for a pastor who serves
alone. But what greater teaching opportunity does the pastor have to
teach and touch the lives of a large number of people?

For the adult teaching ministry to be successful, worship and Sunday
school should not be held at the same time. A number of years ago Gloria
Dei! went to three Sunday morning worship experiences. At 9:45 A.M.,
some members worshipped while Sunday school was held. We noticed
two things. Adult education attendance dropped dramatically, and fewer
children worshipped. We had, in effect, shot ourselves in the foot. We
were subtly teaching our children not to worship and our adults that
Christian education was not important. The next year our schedule
changed to the following: 8:15 A.M., worship; 9:15, worship; 10:15, Sunday school; and 11:15, worship. Worship attendance increased and adult
Sunday School went back to normal.

Weekday Studies

At Gloria Dei! we have something called Tuesday Studies. We offer four
or five, six-week sessions a year. This is the time we do in-depth teaching. Normally we study a book. Seventy-five percent of the books we
study have to do with prayer or some aspect of the spiritual life. The
classes run from 7:30 to 9:00 P.M. and begin with fifteen minutes of
prayer and meditation at 7:15. Prayer needs to be taught. While intercession and petition might seem natural to us, meditation and contemplative
prayer are not. Fortunately, the Christian faith has a rich spiritual history,
and a great number of books have been written on prayer. The following
is a very short bibliography. These books have been road tested, so to
speak. I am sure you have your favorites as well. The key is variety. It is
important to have books for beginners and books for those who are far-
ther along on the faith journey.

Good Places to Begin
Anthony Bloom	*Beginning to Pray*
Dietrich Bonhoeffer	*Life Together*
Grace Brame	*Receptive Prayer*
Richard Foster	*Celebration of Discipline: The Path to Spiritual Growth*
Richard Foster	*Prayer: Finding the Heart's True Home*
O. Hallesby	*Prayer*
George Maloney	*Prayer of the Heart*
Thomas Merton	*Thoughts in Solitude*
Henri Nouwen	*Out of Solitude*
Henri Nouwen	*Reaching Out: The Three Movements of the Spiritual Life*

The Next Step
Anonymous	*The Cloud of Unknowing*
Johann Arndt	*True Christianity*
St. Augustine	*Confessions*
Brother Lawrence	*The Practice of the Presence of God*
Martin Luther	"A Simple Way to Pray" (in *Luther's Works*, vol. 43)
Thomas Merton	*New Seeds of Contemplation*
Percy Parker, ed.	*The Journal of John Wesley*
Brother Ugolino	*The Little Flowers of St. Francis*
Evelyn Underhill	*The Spiritual Life*

Going Deep
St. Bernard of Clairvaux	*Treatise on Loving God*
Walter Hilton	*The Stairway to Perfection*
E. Kadloubousky and E.M. Palmer, trans.	*Writings from the Philokalia on the Prayer of the Heart*
St. Teresa of Avila	*Interior Castle*

Sunday Seminars

Gloria Dei! has a health ministries program. It is staffed part-time by
three members: a parish nurse and two parish counselors. A half dozen
Sunday afternoons a year (and at selected Sunday school hours), they
offer seminars on a variety of health-related issues, relationship building,
parenting, and so forth. Obviously there are other professionals in our
communities besides the pastor who can share their expertise. We should
avail ourselves of their services.

Encouraging Lay-Led Study Groups

Many years ago I visited friends in Arizona. They are members of a
Lutheran church in Sun City. One morning my friend Linda left for a
community Bible study. I asked, "Don't you go to one at church?"
    "Oh, no," she replied. "We don't have one that is lay led. Lutheran
lay people don't get their hands dirty in the Bible. Pastors always lead
the Bible studies."
    Ongoing, lay-led Bible studies are indispensable. People long for
God's healing word. The laity need to learn to read the Bible on their
own. Gloria Dei! has four ongoing Bible studies that meet every week.
While each has a facilitator, the members take turns leading. Each group
has developed its own distinctive personality. One group spends half the
time in prayer and the other half in study. One is scholarly; they have
spent two years on the Gospel of Mark. One group studies at warp speed;
they went through the book of Revelation in six sessions. One is as much
social as it is Bible study. From these groups has emerged our congregational leadership. What an impact they have made. Leaders who come
out of the Bible studies are grounded in faith, rooted in Scripture, and
committed to the church. They have blessed our congregation. Other
study groups can be formed as well. They can include book study and
support groups.

Transforming the Heart

In the spring of 1988, a child in our community was hit by a car and killed. The child was bright, energetic, athletic, and socially outgoing. Now he was dead. The family had just been received into membership, so I officiated at the funeral. The mother had been raised in the Lutheran church. She had attended Sunday School and had been faithful at worship. Unfortunately, the promise of eternal life had never been important to her, and she basically had no depth of understanding concerning it. Each time I was with her, the conversation was similar. Through her wailing laments she would ask, "Is there really a heaven? I want to believe so badly—but I can't. Please assure me that my child is with God." This poor woman not only had to live through her grief, but she also had to do mortal combat with her faith. Her faith did not comfort her. In fact, it had become an affliction for her. And she found no real peace. She had heard the Gospel proclaimed. She knew church doctrine. But she didn't know God—the originator of the promise of eternal life. She moved away about a year after the death, and I have lost touch with her. I pray that she has found some spiritual peace.

The task of the church is to facilitate an active prayer life in our members so God can bind up a grief-laden heart and weave hope in the loom of despair. This woman's Christian education was incomplete. She had learned *about* God, yet she never developed an intimacy *with* God.

Prayer is the living legacy of the church. It is handed down and refined from generation to generation. Clergy, congregations, and families are the keepers of that legacy and share the responsibility for its vibrant existence. Yet we live in a time when spiritually impoverished people are seeking spiritual sustenance and going anywhere it is promised—even outside the faith. To ensure that our spiritual and devotional heritage continues to thrive, we in the church need to augment our efforts to nurture our people spiritually. Our congregations are composed of spiritually illiterate people. While many might know the rudiments of church doctrine, they do not know God. To recall the earlier metaphor, they have a cheese-sandwich faith and need to feast at the banquet table of God's blessings and eat in the supermarket of experiential knowledge.

The apostles begged, "Lord, teach us to pray" (Luke 11:1). People today are pleading for the same thing. Within each of us is a secret self begging to be touched by God. The educational ministry of the church must provide the space, time, and opportunity for God to become our intimate lover and the cherished companion of our hidden hearts.

Retreats

A weekend, directed retreat is an excellent way to foster spiritual growth. It provides an extended period of time for people of faith to gather together in prayer, worship, and discussion. Generally participants know each other and realize that all are in attendance to deepen their life with God. The leader does not have to be the pastor but should have some training in group spiritual work. Many congregations already utilize retreats for couples, youth groups, church governing boards, and the like. A group retreat that centers on the spiritual life can be a powerful experience. The weekend should be designed so there is a time for group prayer and meditation, sessions for discussion, and extended periods of silence. It is also helpful for the leader to be available for the retreatants.

Another kind of retreat is the private retreat. These are very common in the Roman Catholic tradition but rare among Protestants. They are generally made at a Roman Catholic monastery or some retreat center. A private retreat gives time to reflect on your journey with God and to reflect on life as a whole. Generally, monasteries have a guest house with a retreat master whose major responsibility is to insure the comfort and solitude of the retreatants. Private retreats are especially helpful for troubled people who need some spiritual nourishment as well as for those with a deep interest in prayer.

Members of my congregation regularly make private retreats to Holy Cross Abbey, a Cistercian monastery in the Shenandoah Valley of Virginia. While there, they will join in the rhythm of the monks' day and, as they desire, attend worship at the chapel. Once they have been on a private retreat, they go back again and again. Getting them there the first time is what is difficult.

Sample Agenda for a Structured Weekend Retreat

Theme: The Bread of Life

Friday Evening
8:00	Arrive, unpack, settle in
8:30	Evening Prayer (Vespers)
	John 6:22-71: Jesus, the Bread of Life
	Fifteen minutes of silence
9:00	Exegetical work and discussion of the text
10:30	Prayer at the Close of the Day (Compline)
10:45	Social time and sleep

Saturday
9:00	Breakfast (talking allowed)
9:30	Morning Prayer (Matins)
	Reread John 6:22-71 from a different translation
	Fifteen minutes of silence
10:00	Continued discussion of text
10:45	Break
11:00	Lectio (silent, repetitive recitation of the text)
	"I am the bread of life"; or "Jesus is the bread of life"; or "Jesus is the bread of my life"; or something else related to the text.
11:10	Meditatio (reflection on the text)
	What does it mean to be bread?
	What bread sustains my life?
	How was Jesus the bread of life?
	Am I bread to someone else?
11:30	Break before lunch (talking allowed)
12:00	Lunch in silence while someone reads another text related to the subject. For instance, on the theme of the bread of life, portions of Thomas Merton's book *Bread in the Wilderness* could be used.
1:00	Time to read, pray, walk, journal, or visit
2:00	Oratio (oral prayer based on the text)

Confession: We admit that we neglect to be nourished by the bread of life.

Intercession: We remember those who need the bread of life.

Petition: We remember places in our own lives where we need Christ's bread.

Thanksgiving: We give thanks for the bread of life.

Praise: We give God glory for God's mighty deeds.

2:15   Contemplatio

Our silent listening hearts are alone with the bread of life. It might be helpful for the participants to repeat silently "Jesus is the bread of life."

2:45   Break (talking allowed)

3:15   Silent reflection on related biblical texts

Each period of reflection on a text is followed by a brief discussion of that text.

Exodus 16:1-36: Manna in the Wilderness

1 Corinthians 11:17-34: St. Paul on Holy Communion

Matthew 26:17-29: The Last Supper

4:30   Break (in silence)

6:00   Supper (in silence)

8:00   Social time

The breaking of bread ends in a period of joy and fellowship

Sunday

9:00   Breakfast (talking allowed)

9:30   Morning Prayer (Matins)

Discussion of Holy Communion and the bread of life

(You might provide handouts to promote discussion.)

11:00   Closing worship and Holy Communion

12:00   Departure

Quiet Days

A quiet day is simply a one-day retreat. It can be held on a weekday or a Saturday. We have quiet days the first Monday in Advent and the Monday of Holy Week. We always go to a monastery, but quiet days can be held anywhere that engenders some solitude. The purpose is to spend time with God in the company of other Christians. We use two rooms: one is for prayer, meditation, and study; the other is for discussion. Minimal direction is needed. We generally begin with prayer and discussion of the day and end with prayer and Eucharist. A more structured sample quiet-day agenda follows this section.

In the same vein it is a good thing to have a quiet room at church. Sometimes people need a holy place to spend an afternoon or a morning in prayer and reflection. The room should be decorated simply, have an eternal light, a modest altar and cross, a comfortable chair, a Bible, and some devotional books.

Sample Quiet-Day Agenda

Theme: The True Vine - John 15:1-17

8:00	Welcome and description of the day
	Light breakfast (talking allowed)
8:30	Morning Prayer (Matins)
	Five minutes of silence after reading the text
9:00	Exegetical work and discussion of the text
10:00	Break (no talking)
11:00	Lectio (silent, repetitive recitation of the text)
	"I am the true vine"; or "Jesus is the true vine"; or "Jesus is the vine and I am the branch"; or "I abide in the true vine."
11:10	Meditatio (reflection on the text)
	What does it mean to be the true vine?
	How am I attached to the vine?
	How is Jesus the true vine of my life?
	How does Jesus abide in me and I in Jesus?

11:20	Silent reflection on related biblical texts
	Each period of reflection on a text is followed by a brief discussion of that text.
	Isaiah 5:1-7: The Song of the Vineyard
	Galatians 5:22-23: Fruit of the Vine
11:30	Break (talking allowed)
12:00	Lunch in silence while someone reads another text related to the subject. For instance, Howard Thurman's book, *The Centering Moment*, could be used.
1:00	Time to read, pray, walk, journal in silence
2:00	Oratio (oral prayer based on the text)
	Confession: We admit that we do not always abide in the vine.
	Intercession: We remember those who need to be attached to the true vine, Christ.
	Petition: We remember places in our own lives where we need to draw sustenance from the vine stalk.
	Thanksgiving: We give thanks for the vine that gives us hope.
2:15	Contemplatio
	Our silent listening hearts are alone with the true vine that gives us strength and sustains our life. It might be helpful for the participants to repeat silently "Jesus is the true vine of my life."
2:45	Retreat wrap-up and discussion
3:30	Closing worship and Eucharist

Prayer Vigils

A prayer vigil is an exceedingly moving devotional experience, sometimes including both corporate and private prayer. The purpose of the prayer vigil is to provide a continuing and uninterrupted period of communion with God. It includes meditation, periods of silence, prayers that are read, and private prayer. One consequence of the prayer vigil is that the congregation becomes united and centered around discerning the will of God. It is a potent reminder that the purpose of prayer is to be aligned with God's will.

Many congregations hold a prayer vigil that runs continuously from noon on Good Friday until the sunrise worship on Easter Sunday. While Holy Week is a natural time to "watch and pray," prayer vigils on other occasions can be extremely important for the congregation. A prayer vigil can be held before important congregational decisions will be made or at a time of national crisis. We have had prayer vigils before embarking on a building program, when we were getting ready to add staff, and during the Gulf War.

The vigil should include the night hours. The quiet and solitude of a darkened church with only a light at the altar and the eternal light glowing in a corner often engender a sense of the majesty and accessibility of God. Many people actually prefer to pray during the nighttime hours.

Participants should be provided with Bible and other spiritual readings, the church roster so that the entire congregation can be remembered in prayer, and a list of specific prayer requests that have been gathered from the congregation during the weeks before the vigil. Prepared devotional and liturgical materials should be made available, and people are encouraged to take time for private prayer, as well.

The vigil needs to be well planned, organized, and publicized. I suggest putting up the sign-up sheet six weeks before the vigil is scheduled. Half-hour time periods seem to work the best. Very often I hear people comment after the vigil, "This was one of the most powerful moments of my life."

Scheduled Meditation and Prayer

It is important to remind the congregation that "we are a praying community." One way to do that is to schedule specific times (fifteen-minute blocks work well) during the week for prayer and meditation. They might be prior to a class or meeting, at noon, or some other convenient time. They should be led and should include a scripture reading, extrabiblical spiritual reading, and time for silent prayer.

One Lent we asked everyone to spend five minutes in prayer every noon, wherever they were. The congregation worshipped together spiritually even though they were not together physically. It reminded them that the body of Christ is not limited by place or time.

Roots and Branches

When my daughter Kaaren left for college in 1990, I gave her the English translation of *The Christian Life* by Norwegian author Ole Hallesby. In the front of the book was the inscription "To Thomas from Mother and Father, 1935." The book was first used by my grandparents, who gave it to my dad (Thomas),who gave it to me. I in turn passed it on to my daughter. I will pass on to my son Hallesby's book *Prayer*. Those books have instructed four generations of Williamsens for nearly three-quarters of a century. The material in them has helped shape our understanding of the Christian faith. The two books are part of our spiritual roots.

It is helpful for people to come to some understanding about their own spiritual heritage. The Rev. Melissa Mahoney, who works with me at Gloria Dei!, addressed this issue on a recent women's retreat. She had participants draw personal spiritual time lines and then write commentary on their experiences. They began with the faith they learned in their parents' house and at church as children and progressed to the present moment. It proved to be an enlightening and, in a couple of cases, healing exercise.

It is vital that our laity be well educated. They must be armed with knowledge of doctrine and be intimate friends of God. They need this not only for their growth but to be equipped for life outside the walls of the church building. All of us stand on the shoulders of those who have gone before us—for good or for ill. Understanding, cherishing, challenging, discarding, or just studying our own particular religious history can only help us in our growth. Likewise, it is important for people to have an appreciation of their denomination's spirituality and history. Each denomination has rich spiritual writings that helped shape and mold its theology and practice. Periodic classes that use these resources can help people appreciate their own religious inheritance. I say this because many give up on their traditions too quickly and look elsewhere for religious enlightenment.

By the same token, truth comes from many places; no one has a corner on the market. The Christian church has a long and extensive history of providing nourishment for the soul. We begin by understanding our family's tradition, move on to appreciate our denomination's doctrine, and expand our horizons by moving from that solid base to spiritual resources outside our own traditions. Before moving out, however, we need to have a good grasp of our own church's teachings. While there is truth in many places, there is also falsehood and damaging doctrine, and it is important to be able to distinguish between them. It is beneficial for the pastor to be familiar with as much of the historical literature as possible and so to be able to direct people to the literature that would help them the most. It is also important for the pastor to be acquainted with some contemporary authors for the same reason.

CHAPTER 6

Developing Devotional Guides in the Congregation

In 1985 a prominent and beloved member of Gloria Dei! died. He was a charter member and a tireless worker in the church. The entire congregation grieved and deluged the widow with emotional, spiritual, and physical support. A few weeks after the funeral, the widow rose at worship and thanked the congregation for their love and prayers. She said that her faith, strengthened in the midst of a loving congregation, made her grief easier to bear. They were the most poignant words we heard that morning. Her brief statement worked its way into the secret caverns of our hearts. The sermon was anticlimactic. She had made a living testimony to her faith and the importance of Christian community. All theological and spiritual work is contextual. Devotional guides written within the context of a congregational setting encourage members to be diligent in their daily devotions and feed them with the spiritual nourishment provided by friends and pastors.

In 1935 Dietrich Bonhoeffer lived with two dozen theological students in a German underground seminary. This community managed to survive despite the potential threat of imprisonment by the Nazis. Out of that experience Bonhoeffer wrote a wonderful little book entitled *Life Together*. He maintained that it is essential for community health that each person have an active private devotional life. By the same token, he maintained that rich community life and worship feed the individual with spiritual food vital for individual health and well-being. He writes, "Let him who cannot be alone beware of community. Let him who is not in community beware of being alone."[1] The point is well taken. Christian community functions best when it acknowledges that the church is God's creation and its members seek God's guidance through public worship and private devotions.

This chapter's thesis is that devotional guides that are written in the midst of the community's life drama undergird and support each member and strengthen the congregation as a whole. Practically, this chapter is about ways to develop those devotional guides.

Who Writes the Devotional Guides?

Who writes them? The easy answer is, everyone, but not everyone writes at the same time. It depends upon the congregation. At Gloria Dei! I have written most of the devotional guides. I write them because I think of them as extensions of my pastoral ministry. In addition, members have submitted devotions. These were compiled for use in Advent and Lent. We printed a book of prayers written by teens and young children. Individual members have also written guides. One of our members is a poet, and she wrote a book of poetry for use in people's devotional life.

Be creative. Anyone and everyone can be involved at some time. Many congregations produce community-written devotional guides for Advent and Lent. I would also encourage congregations to write guides for use during other seasons as well. Whenever they are used, be assured that they will be appreciated, will be widely used, and will deepen the prayer life of the congregation.

Developing Devotional Guides for Specific Audiences

Congregations are made up of families and individuals who experience joy, sorrow, marriage, grief, illness, worry, doubt, and a myriad of other life situations. For instance, at Gloria Dei! fifteen to twenty infants are born and baptized each year. What if some of the parents who have raised children submitted helpful hints and devotional thoughts for new parents? The collection could be given to the parents on the day of baptism. The African proverb, "It takes a village to raise a child," has become popular in the last few years. Providing devotional guides for parents is one way of doing just that. What a nice gift it could be!

Many of our members become hospitalized during the course of the year. Some of them are children. Suppose the pastors and some selected lay people got together and out of their experiences wrote a book of meditations and scripture readings for people in the hospital. Can you imagine how much people who are struggling with their own illness and disease would appreciate reading about the experiences of others in their congregation and how God can undergird them and walk with them through their time of recuperation?

The list of possible booklets is almost endless. They could include the following: *Thoughts and Prayers as You Get Married, Now that You Are in College, So Your Youngest Child Is Gone, As You Retire, Encouragement as You Look for a Job, Grieving a Miscarriage*, and many others. Pastors, with permission, could share stories from the life of the congregation. Members could narrate personal incidents and provide scriptural texts and prayers that seem appropriate. These booklets could be displayed in a prominent place in the narthex so both members and visitors could use them as needed.

This type of devotional material can be extremely beneficial for members. The guides can undergird people spiritually and provide emotional support in a very poignant and moving way. Guides are a way to provide a ministry of prayer and encouragement in the privacy of people's homes. This is a very practical way for people to minister to each other and encourage each other to pray.

Going On-Line

I must admit I am computer illiterate. Members of my congregation, however, are not. It recently occurred to me that it is possible to provide a ministry to people while they are at work. Many members of our congregation have access to the Internet. A congregation can obtain its own home page or send E-mail to members during the week. The material could include brief scriptural readings, meditations, or prayers, which could be accessed on the computer at any time, day or night.

Our ministry can reach deep into the lives of people where they work and live. Our words can go where we cannot. We can extend our ministry in ways that are limited only by our ability to dream. The congregation is a body of praying believers. The development of materials to enhance people's prayer lives help make that a living reality.

Prayer as Ministry

Mrs. Nagle was as delicate a woman as I had ever met. She was about ninety years old, frail, crippled by arthritis, and plagued by bones so brittle they broke under the slightest stress. In 1970 I was an intern and was instructed to visit her. By all outward appearances, Mrs. Nagle was completely helpless. She was confined to bed in a room that faced the busy Ritchie Highway. I remarked to her, "It must get lonely for you with your daughter away at work all day."

"Oh, no!" she replied. "I have my work."

I was dumbstruck. What work could this fragile, ancient woman do? I thought in my youthful naivete.

"I spend the day in prayer," she began to explain. "When a car goes past I pray for the driver and her family, whoever they are. When children walk under my window on their way to school, I pray that they have a good day and that they mature into fine and faithful adults. I pray for each member of my family—children, grandchildren, great-grandchildren, nieces, and nephews. I pray for the people at church and the leaders of the country. Some days there isn't enough time to get my work all done. No, it's never lonely."

Awe and humility bathed me with an interior cleansing. Mrs. Nagle might have been the most vital person I have ever known. I said, "Mrs. Nagle, I hope my children can play under your window. I can think of no greater ministry than the one you have."

I came to find out that Mrs. Nagle always had been disciplined in her prayer life. Her youth and middle years were just preparatory for her grand ministry of prayer. She was neither useless nor helpless. She was vital and touched the lives of thousands. She was also at peace. She was reaping the reward of a lifetime of prayer. And anyone who was lucky enough to venture into her room or wander past her window was the recipient of God's blessings through her.

There are "Mrs. Nagles"- in-training sitting in the pews of our congregations. Helping them become active men and women of prayer may be the greatest gift they can receive.

CHAPTER 7

Men's and Women's Spirituality

In many ways, writing this book might be more helpful to me than the reader. It has been said, "Teach what you want to learn." Before I began writing, I assessed the strengths and weaknesses of our ministry at Gloria Dei! One of the questions I asked was, How many men participate in those programs designed specifically to encourage a deeper prayer life? Most often men make up only fifteen to twenty percent of the total. I'm not certain I know why that is. One thing I do know is that men tend to attend different kinds of events than women. This chapter might raise as many questions as it answers. Its goal is quite modest: to explore what is most helpful to men and to women as they grow spiritually.

Spirituality and Men

Men do want to grow spiritually. It is a myth to think that they are not as interested in matters of faith as women. Talking about spirituality, however, is not very easy for most men. Let's face it, men carry around a lot of old tapes about religion. Wimps and sissies go to church. "Real guys" play ball, drive fast, and stand on their own two feet. Part of spirituality, indeed a very large part of it, is the confession, I can't do it on my own; I need help. Except when we are sick, we men have a difficult time admitting that we are not totally self-sufficient. Most counselors, psychologists, and psychiatrists I speak with tell me that the vast majority of their patients or clients are women. There is a general unwillingness on the part of men to ask for help. To be a Christian, however, is to acknowledge, I need help!

Some men will speak openly about matters of faith and will attend classes and retreats. Prayer vigils, for some reason, attract a good percentage of men (maybe forty percent). I suspect two of the reasons may be that material is already prepared for them, and the vigil is done privately. Many men must be approached a little differently, though. It is much easier to engage most men in theoretical discussions about creation, the existence of God, or speculative theology than it is to get them to talk about their relationship with God. Given mens' general reluctance to talk about spiritual matters, the best time to speak with a man about matters of faith is usually during a time of crisis, such as divorce, depression, illness, and so forth. Men might not raise the issue, but they do want to know, Is God there? Can God help? With many men, the most effective way to help them grow is to find the appropriate teaching moment and act on it.

A few other guidelines might be helpful for those interested in reaching out specifically to men on their spiritual journeys.

Men generally prefer book studies to Bible studies.

Gloria Dei! has four very active Bible study groups. Two are for women, one is for couples, and one is mixed. We have tried many times to begin a Bible study for men. We failed every time. Men attend weekly Bible studies but only with their wives. Indeed, the couples' Bible study group has grown steadily and men willingly participate. They seem to prefer attending with their wives. This phenomenon is not unique to Gloria Dei! It is true with every other church where I have asked about men in Bible studies.

Men will attend and join a book study group. Men who would seem to be unlikely candidates do not miss a session. In fact, the book study group at Gloria Dei! is mostly men. The books they have studied may not be the most "spiritual," but the men do have to confront their faith in the discussions. They have read, among others, Stephen Covey's *Seven Habits of Highly Effective People* and Scott Peck's *The Road Less Travelled*.

Men like classes that are organized and offer time for discussions.

Experiential learning and talk about matters of the heart are more difficult for men than classes that challenge them intellectually. If you want to touch a man's heart, generally you have to go through the head first. Classes that discuss ethics and morality in an open environment can be stimulating and well attended. During the Persian Gulf War, I taught a five-week class entitled "History of Christians and War." Twenty people showed up; nineteen were men. Discussions were lively and everyone grew a little. I started each class with a scripture reading that lent itself to the evening's topic. We paused for five minutes of silence and ended in prayer. Not too long ago I led a three-week session on biomedical ethics. Men not only attended but participated in the discussion.

One of the keys for helping men grow spiritually is to teach something that has "practical" as well as spiritual value. In the near future we will offer a seminar taught by a physicist on the topic, "The Quest for Truth: Science and Religion in Dialogue." I am confident men will attend because it is a topic that will challenge and inspire them to think.

Men like to eat and need something tangible to do.

Many churches have had very successful prayer breakfasts. The men cook, listen to a speaker, have prayer, and then go home. I know one church that has offered breakfast and prayer at 6:00 A.M. every Wednesday for ten years. The gathering is interdenominational and is supported by a group of churches.

Men are most active in church organizations that *do* things, such as the property committee, ushers, and the like. Many times when they meet, someone offers only a perfunctory prayer at the beginning of the meeting. A nearby Methodist church has turned those meetings, or workdays, into opportunities for spiritual growth. In the middle of the meeting or time of work, participants pause for thirty minutes for worship and Bible study. They break in the middle because attendance is best then. The late-comers have arrived and the early-leavers are still there.

There are opportunities for everyone to grow spiritually. Fostering spiritual growth in the congregation is not only about adding programs, but it should undergird all that is done and take advantage of every opportunity to provide time for worship, Bible study, and prayer.

Nurturing Women's Spirituality

There has been much written on the topic of women's spirituality in recent years. For this book, I have enlisted the help of a very dear friend and graduate of Shalem Institute for Spiritual Direction, the Rev. Katherine Cartwright Knodel, pastor of spiritual care at St. Stephen's Lutheran Church in Wilmington, Delaware.

Many women are struggling to stay active and faithful in the church. Issues of language and patriarchy, however, tend to get in the way. Some women want desperately to be close to God but are not fed fully by our traditional forms and God-talk. The church needs to take the concerns of these women seriously and to engage in some honest soul searching and biblical study. Christian leaders and theologians must learn to proclaim the truth of the Christian message in the context of a new feminism. This section begins that process.

A Beginning

This section is simply a candle that brings light to some of the issues related to nurturing the spiritual lives of women. These issues include language and God-talk, woundedness and healing, and use of the church calendar, the Bible, various contemplative prayer forms, and other resources to help us deepen our relationship with God. I am a Lutheran pastor. I serve in a fairly traditional Lutheran congregation. I have dedicated time to learning about spirituality and to developing events, programs, and literature for use by individuals and groups.

Not everything I write here will resonate with all women. Some men who read this will resonate with it. What I write about language and patriarchy might make some people angry. Some women are not bothered by patriarchy or using only male language for God. Some women are very comfortable with an exclusively male image of God. Our life experiences and relationships form and shape us. Our Christian life in the church as baptized children of God is part of this formation.

Language, Tradition, and Patriarchy

When I was a little girl, no one told me that my opportunities were limited, and so my dreams, hopes, and aspirations included many things that were not traditionally feminine. As I moved into puberty, I began to discover that my opportunities were not as limitless as I had imagined. When I was little, I did not pay much attention to the fact that pastors and acolytes were male. As I entered seventh grade in 1973, I discovered I could not be an acolyte at our church. I wondered why. When no one could provide a reasonable answer—other than, "This is the way it's always been." I became upset. This was my first experience with sexism and I did not like it. It made no sense to me that I could not have the same opportunity as a boy to serve as an acolyte. With the help of my father (who was on church council at the time), we went through the "proper channels" and made changes so that the girls in our congregation would have the same opportunities as the boys. Looking back on this, I chuckle and wish the rest of the sexism and misogyny in the church and in society could be solved so easily.

Sharing leadership means sharing power, and this is very threatening to those who hold the power. Our religious language and traditions, even our very idea of who God is and how we talk about God, have been shaped by patriarchy, a system of power characterized by dominance and submission. It is a system of polarities rather than a system of partnership, where the male dominates the female, the masculine is preferred over the feminine, and the powerless suffer at the hands of the powerful.

Talking about God

How does the church talk about God? When you get right down to it, God is understood as male. "He" has a male son and a male spirit. "He" conceived "his" male child by way of a virgin. We call God "father," "king," "lord," "shepherd." We confess three creeds that identify God the Father, Son, and Holy Spirit-He. In our worship we pray, "Our Father in Heaven...." We casually refer to God-He; it would be unthinkable to speak publicly in most of our churches about God-She, after all, God-She would be a goddess, not "God" at all. Our limited language has little capacity to acknowledge that God is much more than we have created "him" to be.

Language has power. It literally forms our realities and shapes our memories. The limitations of our language and its inability to be precise can have a dramatic affect on how people view reality—themselves, their relationships, their place in the world, and their relationship with God. Take, for example, the word "man." Some people understand this to be an adequate word to describe all of humankind. Personally, I do not hear myself included in that word. How can a word that denotes an adult male connote adults of both genders as well as children? This makes no sense to me.

The interesting thing about the language discussion in the church is that the Bible does not use an exclusively masculine understanding of God. Neither does the Bible insist that only men can serve the Holy One. The Bible affirms God's intention that relationships be conducted with mutuality and that we live our relationships without exploiting another. The Bible challenges us to exercise power as Jesus did, not in physical strength or military might, but in living by God's standards of love and selflessness, not the world's standards of acquisition and power. Only when we can acknowledge that God alone has true control will the dynamics of human relationships change.

The Bible employs a number of metaphors for God. Each one teaches us something important about who God is and how God loves us. Some of these metaphors might be more nurturing than others. Virginia Ramey Mollenkott in her book *The Divine Feminine: The Biblical Imagery of God as Female* (Crossroad Publishing Company, 1984) discusses the challenges of our language and offers a sampling of biblical feminine metaphors for God. The metaphors include God as woman giving birth, nursing mother, midwife, bakerwoman, and *shekinah* ("indwelling presence of God," which in the Hebrew language is a feminine concept).

Many women can trace emotional and spiritual pain to misunderstanding biblical stories and ideas that have been distorted by the lens of patriarchy. The curses of Genesis 3 have often been used to justify dominance of women. In a few cases, the passage has even been used to justify violence against women. I have worked with survivors of spousal abuse who have been told by male pastors and priests to return home and try harder to please their husbands.

What I find compelling in how we talk about God is God's own self-identification in Exodus 3. Moses asks for God's name, and God replies,

"I am who I am." God's self-identification here defies us to limit God with our language. Only God can fathom the entirety of God's own identity. When we give God a name other than the name God chose, our language proves itself to be limiting and imprecise. God's self-identification in the New Testament is revealed in the person of Jesus Christ. What is important about Jesus is his humanity, not his gender. The work that Jesus did, the life he led, his death, resurrection, and continuing presence with us is what we look to.

The "maleness" of God is a large part of our tradition. I cannot imagine Christianity without it, nor would I like to see masculine imagery struck from our religious imagination. We need, however, to understand that God is spirit, that God is neither male nor female, and that being created in God's image has nothing to do with X and Y chromosomes.

Healing and Body Prayer

Many of us are deeply wounded, splintered pieces of a broken humanity. We live in a culture that denies pain and urges us to present a perfect image to the world. Very few of us feel perfect. Many of us have suffered trauma and loss. We hold in our bodies unresolved grief, stress, and anger. We endure headaches, depression, anxiety, muscle tension and aches, tachycardia, angina, stomach upset, ulcers, heart attacks, and cancer, as well as other minor pain or serious disease.

We women often find as we move through our natural biological life cycles that we can become strangers to our constantly changing bodies. From infancy to childhood; to adolescence and the onset of menstruation; for some, to pregnancy and childbirth or miscarriage, breast-feeding and nurturing children; to menopause and the cessation of menstruation, we experience many changes in our bodies. Most of these changes are shrouded in an outwardly imposed secrecy and shame. It is not polite to speak of these things, and few of these experiences are honored in the life of the church.

A third place of disconnection from our bodies occurs as girls begin to mature and develop women's bodies and compare then with the ideal body presented in the media. The problem with the ideal is that it fits less than 10 percent of women. The rest of us spend our lives trying to create a body we can never hope to have and being miserable in the body we do

have. Sometimes this disconnection from our bodies leads to various
eating disorders, including anorexia, bulimia, compulsive eating disor-
der, or ignoring our bodies' needs for healthful nutrition and exercise.

Praying with our bodies can be an incredibly healing response to our
bodies' societal woundings. But body prayer can also be incredibly
threatening. Our bodies hold our secret hurts. Some of these hurts are as
extreme as incest, rape, miscarriage, abortion, stillbirth, or spousal abuse;
in childhood or adolescence we could have been horribly taunted over a
bodily imperfection. I encourage women to be gentle with themselves
and to begin bringing their body into prayer by using something relatively nonthreatening. Some might crave the safety of a group; others will
find work in a group too threatening and will prefer to pray privately.

Breath Prayer

Breath work is a nonthreatening prayer form and the most fundamental
body prayer. No matter what shape your body is in, if you are alive, you
breathe. The purpose of breath prayer is to help you feel connected to
God. Your breath will remind you whose life fills you, how close God is
to you, and that no part of you is beyond God's reach.

I use breath prayer with small groups, as part of pastoral visitation, to
prepare an individual for laying on of hands for healing, or as part of individual confession and absolution. I teach this to people for use in their
own prayer lives, especially during times of crisis or anxiety, when we
feels disconnected with ourselves, or simply as a beautiful way to begin
and end the day.

Begin by making yourself comfortable. Some people like to lie
down, but it is easy to fall asleep in this position; I recommend sitting
with your back erect. Sit in an open position with your hands resting
gently on your legs, palms up. Some people like to touch the tip of their
thumbs to their first or second fingers. Close your eyes. You can memo-
rize the meditation or record it on a cassette tape and then play the tape
back for your prayer time. This meditation is based on Genesis 2:4b-7:

> In the day that the Lord God made the earth and the heavens, when
> one plant of the field had yet sprung up—for the Lord God had not
> caused it to rain upon the earth, and there was no one to till the

ground; but a stream would rise from the earth, and water the whole face of the ground—then the Lord God formed Adam from the dust of the ground, and breathed into his nostrils the breath of life; and Adam became a living being.

(The male language in this account can be difficult for some people. I understand this story in terms discussed by Phyllis Trible in *God and the Rhetoric of Sexuality* [Fortress Press, 1978], where "Adam" refers to our humanity and not specifically to a person of the male gender.)

Breathe deeply, breathe slowly, fill your lungs with air and release it. Breathe in and out ... in and out ... in and out. Recite or hear the scripture text several times. In your mind's eye, see yourself as the dust formed into an empty vessel, and feel God's breath, God's life in and through you.

Continue to breathe as you become aware of your lungs filled with air, with God's own breath and life. Now feel God's breath and life released. Breathe in and out ... in and out ... in and out; feel your body filling with God's own breath and life, releasing God's own breath and life back into the world.

Breathe in God's breath, feeling God's own life in every cell as it passes beyond your lungs and moves through your bloodstream to touch every cell in your body—moving outward be-yond your lungs to and through your heart, spreading through your torso and beyond to your limbs, arms and legs, fingers and toes, up through your shoulders and neck, into and through your head. There is no part of your body God cannot touch, no part of your body that God does not know, no part of your body God has not touched, no part of you God does not see. As you continue to breathe, remember the breath that fills you is God's own breath, God's own life, God's own love.

A period of silence can follow, for the breathing is the prayer. The breathing is the person trusting God and putting her life in God's hands, trusting that God will provide the breath so that her life and God's life in her may continue.

One of my favorite body prayers uses gentle movements to reflect the daily life cycle of the baptized Christian. You may do this with your eyes open or closed.

Begin by visualizing yourself holding your own self, body-mind-spirit, in your own hands at waist level. As you gaze upon yourself there, you pour into that vision all that you are, all that you have experienced, all that troubles you, all that you struggle with. Slowly begin to lift your cupped hands, moving them up-ward along the midvertical line of your body, over your heart, and up. As you do this, see your desire to be present for God, open to God's love and to knowing God. Bring your hands over your face and up over your head, still cupped; open your hands and feel God's life and love filling you and flowing through you, strengthening and supporting you in all you do as you reflect, through arms open to all, God's love in the world. Pause for a moment as your arms are open and you stand as if on a cross. Feel the heaviness of your arms as you rest in God. Continue to bring your arms down. Hold yourself and offer your desire to be present for God to work in and through you, to support and fill you as you empty yourself in service to others.

The meditation continues this way for a period of time and then trails off into silence. The movements continue during a time of silence. When you feel ready, open your eyes and drink in the blessings that surround you and celebrate God, who moves with you constantly and in whom we live and move and have our being.

Laying on of Hands

In my retreat work and during some pastoral care visits, I use laying on of hands for healing an individual's wounds. During a weekend retreat, this contemplative prayer form is set within the service of Holy Communion as the climax of the retreat. Generally, the group sits in a circle with a chair in the middle. I encourage retreat participants to take turns sitting in the chair during the prayers. The entire group lays hands on the person sitting in the chair. The only instruction I give to the retreat participants is to make themselves totally present for God's work through the group. We begin by placing our hands on the person's body while I offer a free prayer and then a period of silence. During this prayer time participants silently rest in God and open themselves to God's life and transforming work. This is a powerful experience of healing and receiving God's embodied grace.

The Church Year and Other Resources

Spirituality is about connecting faith and life with God. Spirituality is like a mirror that reflects our relationship with God. The cycle of the church year is rich with metaphor that relates to the cycles and events of our lives. Within its circle it holds joy and celebration; sadness, sorrow, and suffering; opportunities for new life; the normal and the extraordinary; waiting and expectation; and completion. Our own personal dates of remembrance flesh out the calendar of our inner memory, and we create personal rituals to honor these events in our lives. As an event is held in our memories and honored by ritual, it becomes present to us.

We celebrate the events of our sacred stories year after year so they will become part of the fabric of our lives. Many of our oldest and fondest memories reflect such celebrations. Families pass down to children an identity that includes these celebrations. Our major festivals are Christmas, Holy Week/Easter, and Pentecost. The significance and meaning of other major and minor festivals might vary from place to place, depending on how they are celebrated. A number of relatively obscure Christian festivals and occasions also can be claimed as opportunities for spiritual deepening. I am developing two of these in my current ministry setting.

Holy Saturday. The first is an early morning retreat held the day before Easter. This time is rich in imagery and metaphor, for Jesus was in the tomb. This is a time of deep mystery in our salvation story. The gospel accounts simply state that Jesus was laid in the tomb and sealed in with a stone. We also know that the tomb was guarded. What went on inside remains a mystery, but we know that the tomb is a place of metamorphosis and transformation. Ancient people often buried their dead in caves, considered to be the womb of the Great Mother. Geodes exemplify the mystery of what goes on deep in the earth. On the outside, the geode appears to be an ordinary stone, rough and earth-toned; break it open and explore a depth of endless beauty with clear-colored crystal formations in unique designs encrusting the hollow stone. I have given participants in this event a small geode as a reminder of this metaphor for the work of the Spirit and transformation in life of the believer. In the tomb, God worked as in the womb, bringing forth new life—a resurrected Jesus. It is a new reality unlike any we could have imagined.

The retreat can be structured in many ways and offers tremendous opportunities for birthing creativity. The first year I offered the retreat, it was structured around bread baking. We planned to bake bread and use our process as a metaphor for life in the Spirit. The bread was shared at the Easter Vigil and Resurrection Day services. An abundance of gorgeous metaphor shaped the retreat, and that is okay if you are interested in exploring a variety of metaphors. I prefer to explore one metaphor in depth. The wonderful fruit of this retreat is that as you gather year after year, you develop a deep space that is present for God's work of growth and transformation within you. Rather than experiencing only the silence of the tomb, you experience the quiet activity of death before the bursting forth of new life. This rhythm is also ideal for a personal retreat.

The Visitation. The second event I have been working with is a celebration of the Visitation (May 31, Luke 1:39-47). This can be an occasion for women to gather at the church or at someone's home to celebrate what God calls each of us to birth in the world. The fruits of our labors might include children, projects, ministries, anything that God has called into being through our work and discipleship. I hosted an informal gathering around a potluck meal. I read the scripture text and encouraged conversation and prayer. This gospel story is filled with beautiful imagery about women's discipleship, and we celebrated what God was doing through each of us. This idea can be brought to life in many ways. It could be used as an opportunity for a day-long or weekend retreat. The time could be built around conversation or contemplation. There could be an interplay of the two. Imagine contemplative arts and crafts that draw us into the tradition of icon creation, where the crafting of art is the prayer and the finished piece a window to God.

Other ideas for celebration in the church year include:

The Holy Innocents: December 28, Matthew 2:13-18
The Annunciation: March 25, Luke 1:26-38
The Nativity of John the Baptist: June 24, Luke 1:57-67 (68-80)
St. Mary Magdalene: July 22, John 20:1-2, 11-18
Mary, the Mother of Jesus: August 15, Luke 1:46-55

Feminine biblical imagery for God and biblical metaphors such as the wilderness, the desert, liberation from slavery, wrestling with God (Jacob at the Jabbok), Jesus' "I am ..." sayings from John's gospel,

Psalms 131 and 139:13-16, and Philippians 2:5-11 can be used to build retreats or classes. Women can also gather in celebration of God's indwelling Spirit as witnessed to be saints, martyrs, renewers of the church, renewers of society, and Christian mystics.

These ideas should relate to events in our lives, so these stories become a connection God makes with us. Part of the work of an event based on these celebrations can be searching the Scriptures for more stories about people such as Mary Magdalene or Mary the Mother of Jesus, or for stories about women who figure in Paul's letters, the gospel accounts, or the Old Testament.

Look at these stories through the lens of God's love in the person of Jesus. Martin Luther described John 3:16 as the Gospel in miniature: "For God so loved the world that he gave his only Son, so that everyone who believes in him may not perish but have eternal life." Looking at the Scriptures through this lens might help some women make peace with the language issues and encounter God in stories that bring with them the possibility of new life.

For Further Reading

Edwards, Tilden H. *Spiritual Friend.* New York: Paulist Press, 1980.

Fischer. Kathleen. *Women at the Well: Feminist Perspectives on Spiritual Direction.* Mahwah, N.J.: Paulist Press, 1988.

Keating, Thomas. *Open Mind, Open Heart: The Contemplative Dimension of the Gospel.* Rockfort, Mass.: Element, Inc.,1986.

Laffey, Alice L. *An Introduction to the Old Testament: A Feminist Perspective.* Philadelphia: Fortress Press, 1988.

Mollenkott, Virginia Ramey. *The Divine Feminine: The Biblical Imagery of God as Female.* New York: Crossroad, 1984.

Morley, Janet. *All Desires Known: Prayers Uniting Faith and Feminism.* Wilton, Conn.: Morehouse-Barlow Co., Inc., 1988.

Morton, Nelle. *The Journey Is Home.* Boston: Beacon Press, 1985.

Osiek, Carolyn. *Beyond Anger: On Being a Feminist in the Church.* Mahwah, N.J.: Paulist Press, 1986.

Schussler Fiorenza, Elisabeth. *In Memory of Her: A Feminist Reconstruction of Christian Origins.* New York: Crossroad Publishing, 1989.

Smith, Martin L. *The Word Is Very Near You*. Cambridge, Mass.:
    Cowley Publishers, 1989.
Trible, Phyllis. *God and the Rhetoric of Sexuality*. Philadelphia: Fortress
    Press, 1978.
Trible, Phyllis. *Texts of Terror: Literary Feminist Readings of Biblical
    Narratives*. Philadelphia: Fortress Press, 1984.
Wuellner, Flora Slosson. *Prayer and Our Bodies*. Nashville: The Upper
    Room, 1987.
With One Voice: A Lutheran Resource for Worship. Minneapolis:
    Augsburg Fortress, 1995. (Some hymns that use feminine and other
    nontraditional images and language are included in this worship
    resource and can be used as devotional aids.)

CHAPTER 8

Sharing Our Spiritual Legacy: Children and Spiritual Growth

Suffer the little children to come unto me, and forbid them not; for of such is the kingdom of heaven. And he took them up in his arms, put his hands upon them, and blessed them

—Matthew 19:14, 15

When my five-year-old son, Erik, developed diabetes, it was a blow to our entire family. A week after we discovered the disease, I called a friend to go for a noon jog and talk. As we were running he said, "Don't let Erik be passive in his illness."

"What in the world are you talking about? Erik needs to accept that he has diabetes," I shot back.

My friend Roy replied, "No, I mean don't let him be spiritually passive. Help him to take control of his disease spiritually." He then proceeded to give me a few practical suggestions.

After I shared this conversation with my wife, Faye, we sat down with Erik. We told him that Jesus did not want him to have diabetes. We said, "Jesus might heal you. Jesus might not heal you. Either way, Jesus cares that you are sick and he will be with you." We then showed him a picture of his pancreas and described the beta cells that produce insulin. We told him that this is the part of his body that was not working right. We then said that every night all of us—Faye, my daughter, Kaaren, Erik, and I—would picture Jesus in his pancreas. Erik thought this was okay. Every night before Erik went to bed, we would pray and then for five minutes or so we would visualize Jesus in Erik's pancreas. We called it "doing your pancreas." We did this faithfully for months. Erik said he pictured Jesus with a pin trying to get the insulin out of his pancreas.

After about three months Erik said, "Jesus moved from my pancreas to my heart. I like him there." After about six months Erik told me, "I finally figured it out, Dad. Jesus didn't want me to have diabetes. My body just let me down." That deep understanding gave Erik peace. It was a gift from God to a little boy. It was the fruit of prayer. Erik "did his pancreas" for many years. He is twenty now and a spiritually rich person. I am convinced that Erik's active prayer life helped him mature into the person he is. I would never wish illness on anyone. The truth is, however, that God was able to use Erik's illness for good and that his spiritual discipline helped him become spiritually mature and emotionally whole.

Such is the legacy I wish for all our children. When new members join Gloria Dei! I tell them I want three things for their children. I want them to know that their pastors love them, so when they grow up and move to Texas or North Dakota and need help, maybe they will say, Hey, "I remember that pastor at Gloria Dei! He was a good guy. Maybe I can talk to a pastor."

I want them to know that the church cares for them and is a nurturing place. Then, when they mature and move to Seattle or Phoenix, one of the first things they will think is, "I need to find a church. I need to be in a place that provides for my spiritual and emotional well-being."

Finally, I want them to have learned from the pastors and congregation that wherever they go, their God will already be there to greet them, love them, sustain them, and hold them like a shepherd cradles his sheep. Then, when they become adults and move to Bosnia or Cairo, they can say, "I know that God will be with me. I can go to the quiet place of my heart and God will be there to surround me with love."

Sadly, not all of our children at Gloria Dei! learn those things. Yet, like you, we strive to make it a reality for as many as we can and turn the rest over to God's gracious care. This chapter is about doing spiritual ministry with children and teens. Parents need help. It is hard to be a parent today. It is harder to be a child.

Sunday School Teachers

In 1969 Joe Namath, alias "Broadway Joe," turned the football world upside down by leading his New York Jets to victory over the legendary

Johnny Unitas and his Baltimore Colts. Joe Namath had a reputation as a party-goer and man about town. When he purchased a restaurant in New York that was frequented by unsavory characters and big-time gamblers, no one was surprised. At the time, the commissioner of the National Football League was Pete Rozelle. Rozelle told Namath to sell the restaurant because it tarnished the image of the NFL. Namath refused. Rozelle, however, would not relent in his insistence that Namath sell. A confrontation was inevitable. Suddenly Namath called a news conference. He announced, "I have changed my mind. I will sell."

The media were dumbfounded. They insisted on an answer. "Why are you selling?"

"I remember a lesson my Sunday school teacher taught me," was the reply. He then left the interview room.

Next to parents and a few select relatives, Sunday school teachers have the most lasting impact on the religious and spiritual training of children. Children learn more about religion by what they see and experience than by what they are taught. Sunday school teachers not only teach lessons, they teach life by example.

Churches need to be discerning when asking people to teach Sunday school. The teachers are the unsung heroes of the church. They can help children learn to pray. They help shape a child's impression of the church. They can lay the foundation for Christian witness and service. (We also should be careful when selecting material that is used because some Sunday school material is legalistic and moralistic.)

Children and Devotions

The gift of prayer is a special present. It will survive through our children. In fact, prayer is a sacred trust given to us with the understanding that we share it with our children. But this is an area where most parents need help. Parents are the ones who shape a child's devotional life. Generally speaking, parents will teach what they were taught by their parents. Some parents have a strong family history of having devotions. I am afraid, however, that most do not. Parents normally have good intentions but fail in helping their children learn to pray because they themselves have a difficult time with prayer. Consequently, the best way for a congregation to help children learn to pray is to teach and encourage the parents to pray. In addition, the church should itself be a spiritual model for children. For example, every youth activity should begin with scriptural reading, a brief meditation, and prayer.

Congregations can also help parents by providing materials to use with children. Most children love it when parents read to them, and there are some wonderful resources available. Bibles with pictures tell the history of God's saving actions for humankind in ways that will remain with the child forever. Likewise, many religious storybooks tell stories about Christian heroes. Some contemporary fiction paints pictures of God with words and stories. All these resources help shape a child's image of God.

Devotional guides provide a framework for daily devotions and help children get in the habit of daily prayer. I have written a book entitled *Five Minutes with God: Daily Devotions for Parents and Children*[1] with a brief scriptural reading, a thought for discussion, and a prayer. Similar resources are available from many Christian publishers. A book fair is an excellent way to help parents choose appropriate books and videos to use with their children. These books should be screened by the pastor for content and by an elementary school teacher for age suitability.

Children at Sunday Worship

Children and teens belong in Sunday worship. I realize they can be disruptive, but how else do we teach children to worship except by encouraging them to worship? They also need to be included in the worship service. Ways for them to participate are endless. They can acolyte; help usher; sing in the church choir, children's choir, or youth choir; and do sacred dance.

I like the children's sermon. I understand that children's sermons are controversial in some places because they are used to moralize or entertain the adults, and it is true that often the sermons are not developmentally age appropriate, but I think they are a vital component of ministry with children. The children's sermon is a time to talk about the love of God. It is a time to cherish the children and a time to remind them that God is always with them. It is a time to be with the children and tell the story of God in a loving and nurturing atmosphere.

Not too long ago I left out the children's sermon because of a time problem. After we had sung the last hymn, a little girl turned to her mother and said, "Church isn't over yet, Mom."

"Yes, it is dear," her mom replied.

"No, it isn't. We didn't get to go up front," the little girl patiently explained to her mother.

The average age of people in the United States is thirty-one. The average age of people in the mainline denominations is fifty-one. That is a very sad statistic. If we are to change the present trend of a graying church, we will need to gear our worship so everyone, adults and children, can be touched and taught spiritually.

Youth Bible Studies

Teens live in a world that questions religious values and long-held Christian truths. Many teens would like to have faith, but questions get in the way. Pastor Mahoney, the other pastor at Gloria Dei!, has started a weeknight Bible study for youth. It started slowly. Indeed, for a year it looked doomed. Nonetheless, she persevered. Today it is an active group of ten to twelve that meets in her office every Wednesday evening for study, supper, and conversation. It is an informal time when she and a lay leader can listen to questions, help the teens to answer the questions themselves, and encourage them to think theologically. A number of Bibles have annotations and questions suitable for teens. Any Christian bookstore should keep them in stock.

Mothers' Prayer Chain

Wednesday at Gloria Dei! is music rehearsal evening. The choirs and sacred dance troupes practice from 4:30 P.M. until 7:00. At 6:00 they eat together. It is a great time for the children and the scheduling works well for the parents because they only have to bring their children out once a week. The church is like a three-ringed circus with activities everywhere and constant noise, but the enterprise is well worth the effort.

Now, imagine in the midst of this cacophony a group of women sitting quietly in a room. They are praying. They are praying for the children practicing. They are praying for specific children who are ill or troubled or sad. They are praying for children in Bosnia and inner cities. This is the mothers' prayer chain. It works like a regular prayer chain:

The mothers receive requests for prayer at home from the pastors, parents, or the children themselves, and they pray for the children individually as requests come in. Some of the mothers set aside time every day and offer prayers beyond those requested, and all the mothers pray as a group on Wednesday. They send notes to children telling them they are being remembered in prayer. It is not a ministry that is very visible. Yet these prayers are like arms stretched out to our children to support and carry them through hard times.

Family Devotions: A Lost Art?

Many of us grew up in homes that had a strong family devotional heritage. My family had devotions after supper every evening. My mom or dad would read a biblical text, share some thoughts about it, and encourage my sister and me to comment on the text and its applications in our life. At bedtime my mother would be certain we read the Bible and said our prayers. It was as routine as brushing our teeth. I always thought that when I had children, I would do the same. Something happened. When our children were small, we indeed had family devotions. As they grew, we had few family meals and fewer family devotions. When we tucked them in bed we would pray with them, but the older they got the less often we tucked them in bed. By the time they were in sixth grade, family devotions became almost nonexistent. Each child had his or her own devotions, but we seldom had them as a family.

My children are grown now, and it saddens me that I didn't give my children a stronger example for doing family devotions. I have discovered, however, that what I experienced is not at all unusual. Many families in our congregations have good intentions but fail to have regular family devotions. It is difficult for individuals to find time for devotions. It becomes even more problematic for families to find time together. It is, however, important enough for congregations to address the issue.

Family devotions can be a natural part of the day. Most families are able to find some time during the course of the day when they can gather for prayer. It may be at a meal, before bedtime, or at bedtime. I know one family that has decided the supper hour devotions will not be violated by sports, meetings, work, or the phone. After devotions they have family discussions about politics, sports, and other topics.

Some families find it easier to have family devotions during Advent. It is a good time for congregations to encourage the practice. Most denominational publishing houses have very good devotional books for Advent that use Advent calendars, candles, and other visual helps.

Sometimes encouraging family devotions seems like a lost cause. Nonetheless, we persevere. We never know when someone will be touched.

A Few Parting Thoughts

Children learn more by what they see and experience than by what they are told. When I was organizing Gloria Dei!, I visited many people who said something like, "I don't go to church any more. My mother dragged me there too often when I was a child. I don't ever want to go back." I heard something similar to that so frequently that I decided to explore that statement a little further. I wanted to know what happened when they arrived at church. What I discovered was extremely instructive. They all said they were taught *about* love. They were not, however, treated lovingly. "Don't run." "Sit still! Don't you know this is God's house?" Pastors were distant and adults were domineering. They grew up learning that "church is a place that makes me feel bad."

If we want our children to know and experience the gracious love of God, we must be certain that first they experience human love in our churches.

CHAPTER 9

Thoughts about Worship

*To worship is to quicken the conscience by the holiness of God, to
feed the mind with the truth of God, to purge the imagination by the
beauty of God, to open the heart to the love of God, to devote the
will to the purpose of God.*

—William Temple

In 1981, the nation's air traffic controllers went out on strike. As a result,
air safety became a concern. The federal government demanded that air
traffic controllers return to work. They refused. A bitter court battle en-
sured. Members of my congregation outside Washington, D.C., included
a striking air traffic controller in peril of losing his job and one of the
leading attorneys prosecuting the case for the National Labor Relations
Board. They did not, however, know each other. One Sunday morning I
looked up, and to my amazement, they were sitting in the same row. I
thought to myself, "A Christian church is a place where people of differing ideologies can worship together in harmony." After worship I
introduced the two "opponents." I was hoping they would see the spiritual ties that united them and set aside any differences. One did. One
could not. The meeting was cordial but very tense. I am sure lunchtime
discussion was very interesting at each house.

A wise old pastor once told me, "Church is the place where the
person you want to worship with the least, sings in the choir." It would
be grand if everyone in the church actually liked each other. It does not
work that way. What makes worship such an other-worldly event is that
people who won't even speak with each other can participate in the act
of worshipping their God. People with diametrically opposing political

viewpoints will sing the same hymn. Is it hypocritical? Maybe. It also points out a deep spiritual truth: Something happens in corporate public worship that cannot occur anywhere else. For a few moments we become the body of Christ. We touch a spiritual reality in the act of worship. And we are touched, in the act of worship, by a divine presence. Let me illustrate.

Emily Shiflet had recently joined Gloria Dei! She was a life-long Christian and possessed a deep and abiding faith. She was also dying of brain cancer. Her duel with cancer was valiant. Her indomitable spirit inspired her family and left the congregation in awe. Her surgeries were numerous, and recuperation was long and drawn out. One Sunday, the day after she was released from the hospital after her last surgery during the time when the congregation shares joys, her husband, Roy, wheeled her into church. She was too weak to speak. Roy spoke for her. "She made me bring her," he said. "She had to worship with the congregation today."

Corporate worship has the power to bind, even for a brief time, broken relationships. Worship's healing touch mends the broken heart and lifts the downcast spirit. It inspires the soul to soar in love and catches the breath of God so we breathe the air of hope and forgiveness. It celebrates the mystery of God's active presence in each of us. It is an act whereby the worshippers are acted upon.

Worship will at different times inspire, challenge, motivate, cause parishioners to think, educate, irritate, touch deeply, move to laughter and tears, and so forth. The content and form of the music, the liturgy, the lessons, the prayers, sacraments, and the sermon all converge to deepen people's faith and advance spiritual growth. Worship should provide time for corporate praise and prayer and private reflection and meditation.

This chapter begins the task of addressing the question, How can our worship inspire, foster, and encourage spiritual growth? Here we will briefly examine ways to use music, liturgy, lessons, and silence to touch the secret places of the heart.

The Worship Leader

Sunday worship for the pastor, assisting minister, lector, musicians, ushers, altar guild, and acolytes begins Saturday night—or sooner. In order to lead worship, our hearts must be prepared. The congregation knows when the participants are only going through the motions. Worship demands that the leaders take time for confession, intercession, and petition. It means asking God to use us as instruments of grace. To be spiritually prepared to lead worship means being receptive to God's spirit moving through us. It begins Saturday when we prepare for sleep. We pray, "Lord God, tomorrow I lead worship. Use my skills to touch someone. Use my words to increase another's faith. Forgive my sins. Help me to sleep restfully and peacefully in your arms. Amen." Sunday morning, before worship, we pray a similar prayer. I read Luther's Sacristy Prayer and spend fifteen minutes in silent contemplation.

> O Lord God..., be my helper and let your holy angels attend me. Then if you are pleased to accomplish anything through me to your glory and not to mine or to the praise of others, grant me out of your pure grace and mercy, a right understanding of your word and that I may also diligently perform it.

Liturgy

The Sunday liturgy is the church's public worship. This worship is a holy gathering of individuals and families who have worshipped separately all week. At worship we participate in the salvation history of the world. We stand on the shoulders of those who have gone before us to proclaim God's salvation to the assembled and to serve as a foundation for those who will come after us. Jesus, in his High Priestly Prayer in John 17, breathes insight into the purpose of our worship. As he was preparing for death, Jesus prayed to his Father, "I have made your name known ... so that they may be one" (vv. 6,11). His prayer is also for the future: "I ask not only on behalf of those but also on behalf of those who will believe in me through their word" (v. 20).

First and foremost, we gather for worship to give glory and honor to God and through prayer, praise, and thanksgiving "to make God's name known." Additionally, community worship builds up the faith of the people and allows them to peer into the mystery of God's presence in their lives. God does not need our worship. The people, however, do. God is all in all and quite able to live without our adoration. We offer it because we love God and cannot keep our praise silent. Although God can live without us, Christians cannot live without God. African American author Richard Wright says of the black church, "Worship is the place we dip our poor tired bodies in the cool springs of hope."[1] Karl Meninger wrote in his book *Whatever Became of Sin* that of all the professions, clergy have the greatest opportunity to heal or make whole by sharing words of forgiveness and the promises of God.[2]

Worship at its best allows the silent, attentive heart to encounter God's presence, discover its truest being, and see others as equal members of the body of Christ. We become aligned with God's will and discover our unique place in God's kingdom. We are touched by the transcendent God who stoops down to raise us to new levels of sanctity, and we are permeated with the immanent God who captures our hearts and surrounds them in a vigil of love.

Forms of Liturgy

The liturgy is an aesthetic expression of our love for God. The word "liturgy" comes from two Greek words—*leiton*, which means "pertaining to the people," and *ergon*, which means "work." For the Greeks, liturgy was any work or service rendered to the community for the common good. Christians and Jews alike employed the term to designate their worship. St. Paul calls himself "a liturgist [*leitourgion*] of Christ to the Gentiles" (Romans 15:16). Whenever the church as the people of God gathers together in prayer, we have liturgy. The form the liturgy takes should reflect two concerns: (1) the denomination's liturgical tradition and its spiritual heritage because we do stand with Christians of all time in our worship; and (2) the traditions and life stories of the people served.

In many denominations the debate rages over "contemporary worship forms." The liturgy is servant to the purpose of worship. The form it takes must have substance for the people who use it and be meaningful for visitors and new members as well. It is a good idea to vary the form and music used. It should take into account the age of the congregation, the educational level, the setting (urban, rural), the major concerns of the community, and so on. For it to be truly public worship, it should serve the public spiritually and in a form they understand. If a particular worship style nurtures the people and the pastor dislikes it—too bad. Better that way than what I see too often: pastors in the name of "liturgical renewal" wounding the worship practices of a community. That does not mean that anything goes, but it does mean that the form is secondary to the purpose of building up the faith of the people and becoming aligned with God's will.

We are living in a time of the church's history when the liturgy and its forms are being hotly contested. I attended a bishop's convocation in my synod a few years ago, and the subject came up. One pastor categorically stated, "I would rather have my church half empty and use our correct liturgy than have the church full and use one of those new liturgies." In his case, the liturgy was not servant of worship but an inviolate form to cling to and protect. Worship always changes. We just need to worship in such a way that God is praised, the sacrament celebrated, the word preached, and the people of God built up.

Be creative. Be innovative. Dare to risk. Dare to fail. But let the liturgy be the living work of the people of God.

Music: A Few Thoughts

Of all the artistic gifts God has given, music may be the greatest. It is certainly the most accessible. The airwaves are filled with song. Tone-deaf people sing lustily in showers across the planet. Even when the words are in a foreign language, the music can affect us deeply. One does not have to understand German to be moved by the chorus of Beethoven's Ninth Symphony. The church has a long and illustrious history of supporting composers of music that portrays life from the heights of ecstatic worship to the depths of desperate searching for God and peace. Musical tastes vary as much as the music styles and forms themselves. Christian worship should employ many differing musical idioms. The purpose of music is not to entertain but to build up the faith of the people.

Chants, plain songs, and psalm tones have been part of Christian worship almost since the beginning. The music's soft and flowing tones are sung from deep within us. While this music does not seem to be popular with many contemporary Christians, its quiet and meditative texture can touch us in ways other music cannot. During Communion it can be spiritually enriching for the congregation to sing brief, meditative chants and songs. Recently I have been using chants from the community at Taizé. They are very singable and encourage quiet reflection.

Almost everyone loves to sing "Silent Night" on Christmas Eve. Its simple beauty suggests in turn the simplicity of the stable and recollects for us the Christmases of our youth. A less popular Christmas carol is "Of the Father's Love Begotten." It is a plain song meant to be sung in a free-flowing, meditative manner. While "Silent Night" touches our heart, "Of the Father's Love Begotten" helps us look deep in our spirits for the love God birthed in us. A steady diet of plain songs may bore many in our congregations. Coupled, however, with other popular hymns, they can add immensely to worship.

Popular music can also be adapted and the words rewritten to express deep spiritual truths. For instance, Lionel Richie's song "Hello, Is It Me You're Looking For?" was written as a love song. It can, however, easily be adapted and arranged to suggest that God is singing it to a world looking for the holy. "Hello! Is it me (God) you're looking for?" Many people know the song and its message can be powerful.

Years ago I was taught that there are two types of music: sacred and secular. Those are false distinctions. There are, indeed, two kinds of music: good and bad. Music of all kinds sets the tone and can touch the deepest and most secret places or our inmost selves.

Corporate Prayer and the Use of Silence

That prayer should be central to every liturgy is obvious. Worship begins with prayerful confession, moves through the prayer in the Kyrie and Gloria, the responses to the lessons, the prayer of the day, and the pastoral prayer or the prayer of the church. If possible, provide time for silent reflection and private prayer during parts of the liturgy, for example, during the confession, after the lessons, and after the sermon. Too often congregations rush through worship and leave little time for silence. We are guilty of that at Gloria Dei!, to be sure. Silence, however, is a gift we

can give the congregation. Sometimes it is best to provide time for silence at evening worship during the week or at a time when parents will
not have to worry about children. Or maybe we can teach our children
the value of a few moments of silent prayer, as difficult as that might
seem to a four-year-old who wiggles like a puppet on a vibrating string.

Many congregations share joys and concerns at worship. This sharing becomes the raw material for the pastoral prayer. In a very real sense
the congregation sets the agenda for the prayer. The sharing of joys and
concerns serves many functions. It furnishes information, affords members the opportunity to care for each other, and provides a healing place
to share the pain or express the joy. I find it best to share joys and concerns at separate times. Once a person shares a concern, people are generally reluctant to share a joy. These joys and concerns can be posted on
a bulletin board in the narthex so people who attend another service, or
who missed worship, can be made aware of what is going on in people's
lives. I am always amazed and gratified by the number of people who
call or write a note to someone who has shared a concern. This arena
provides a marvelous opportunity to encourage mutual ministry to take
place. And allowing silence during the prayer of the church gives worshippers the opportunity to respond with their own silent petitions on
behalf of those who have shared.

CHAPTER 10

Keepers of Solitude

A number of years ago a fifty-year-old executive attended a series of classes I was teaching. Before each class, we would meditate for twenty minutes. During class the man listened attentively but seldom participated in discussion. When the last class was completed, the man rather sheepishly confided, "I enjoyed the course, but I really came to participate in the silence."

Each week a half dozen women gather to pray. Before they pray aloud, they spend ten minutes or so in silence.

Every month a parishioner comes in to discuss her spiritual life. We meet for ninety minutes. The first thirty minutes are spent in silent prayer.

What is this need for silence? Is it just to escape the phone for a while? Is it to "get away from it all" for a fleeting moment? Is it to find a peaceful place? I would say, on the surface, yes to all these things. I think there are deeper reasons, as well. Instinctively we know that there are fruits in interior silence and solitude. For the Christian there is also the realization that God whispers into the silent listening heart. In addition to our natural inclination for community, we need silence—time for hushed dialogue with God. Built into the human condition is an inner place that cries out for God and yearns for one-on-one contact with the holy. St. Augustine of Hippo wrote in the fourth century, "Lord, you have created us for yourself and our hearts are restless till they rest in you."[1] The restless heart, however, does not always know where to seek rest.

Many people look in all the wrong places to comfort a restless heart. We distract ourselves with a procession of sounds and unremitting noise. Elevators blare out music. People on the telephone are put on hold and must endure Muzak or an intrusive commercial. Commuters on trains and joggers on the street pass the time with headphones strapped to their heads. We use this cacophony to fill the empty soul and hide our spiritual poverty. There is little silence anywhere. In fact, silence is feared. Studies have shown that if there is more than fifteen seconds of silence in a group, someone will speak. Churches, unfortunately, tend to reflect society's need for distractions. At Gloria Dei! we occasionally become so pressed for time when we worship that we not only fail to make room for silence, we rush the end of the liturgy so the next service can begin on time. Compounding the problem, congregations keep members busy with committee work, working on this cause or that project. As Parker Palmer once declared, "Too often the church is the enemy of our solitude." That is an unfortunate truth, and churches must begin to take seriously their role as keepers of the solitude. Jesus said, "Come to me...and I will give you rest" (Matthew 11:28) and "Is it not written, 'My house shall be called a house of prayer....'" (Mark 11:17). Projects are good and committees are necessary, and we need to do more. Actually, we might need to do less.

God comes to us in silence, for God's presence is not always easy to detect. Jesus began his public ministry by spending forty days of solitude in the wilderness. He regularly left the twelve to pray alone in silence. The story of Elijah, the prophet, dramatically illustrates God's tendency toward subtle manifestation. When Jezebel heard that Elijah had killed all the prophets of Baal, she "took out a contract" on Elijah. Elijah fled in fear. Eventually he ended up in a cave on Mount Horeb, another name for Mount Sinai, the Mountain of the Lord. On the mountain before the Lord, God said to Elijah,"Go out and stand, for the Lord is about to pass by" (1 Kings 19:11). Centuries before, when Moses ascended the same mountain to receive the law, God appeared on the mountain in a dense cloud and in thunder and lightning and "Mount Sinai was wrapped in smoke because the Lord had ascended upon it in fire; the smoke went up like the smoke of a kiln, while the whole mountain shook violently" (Exodus 19:18). The narrative in Kings describes a different kind of theophany.

> Now there was a great wind, so strong that it was splitting mountains and breaking rocks in pieces before the Lord, but the Lord was not in the wind; and after the wind an earthquake, but the Lord was

not in the earthquake; and after the earthquake a fire, but the Lord
was not in the fire; and after the fire a sound of sheer silence. When
Elijah heard it, he wrapped his face in his mantle and went out and
stood at the entrance of the cave. Then there came a voice to him....
                                                    —1 Kings 19:11b-13b

Isaiah understood love of "sheer silence" when he wrote, "In re-
turning and rest you shall be saved; in quietness and trust shall be your
strength" (Isaiah 30:15). The point of all this is that a growing intimacy
with God demands times of silence. Thomas Merton wrote, "There is a
silent self within us whose presence is disturbed precisely because it is
so silent: It can't be spoken. It has to remain silent."[2] It is to this "silent
self" that God reveals God's self. This does not mean that God is not
revealed in other ways as well. It does mean, however, that we come to
know God more intimately and love God more fervently when we give
God the space, time, and opportunity to come to us in our silent secret
heart. Silence is essential for the life of faith and our most personal meetings with God.

This quiet, prayerful encounter with God is not for us alone. We not
only grow in faith, we also grow in love. Mother Teresa said, "Prayer
enlarges the heart."[3] Silence helps us hear the heart of another's whis-
pered pain. Silence helps us be attentive to the world's wounded, who
have no voice. It is when we are still and attentive that God can transform our hearts and we become a new creation.

Ancient Egyptians used to weigh the hearts of the dead. The heart
was the measure of courage and love. It rings true. If Mother Teresa is
correct, then there are not scales large enough to weigh the heart of a
lifelong Christian who receives God into the stilled and quiet heart.

"Well, that's a nice homily. But what are we to do in the congregation that's practical and achievable?

Obviously that is what much of this book is about. But specifically
regarding silence, I think we can do two things.

1. Gather a small group of people who are interested in the subject
   of prayer and meet weekly for one month. Spend the time in
   silent prayer together. After one month of prayerful reflection,
   begin to discuss ways silence can be fostered in worship, committee meetings, staff meetings, and specially scheduled worship and
   prayer times during the week.

2. Preach a series of sermons on silence or the church as keeper of the solitude or a related subject. People will hear the truth in it. Two good books to use as resources are Henri Nouwen's *Reaching Out* or Dietrich Bonhoeffer's *Life Together*.

PART 3

Spiritual Leaders

CHAPTER 11

Spiritually Grounded Lay Leadership

How very good and pleasant it is when kindred live together in unity!

(Psalm 133:1)

Unity in the community of the church does not happen by chance. It is the result of pastors, church board, paid staff, and key lay leaders agreeing on a vision of ministry, understanding that the church is not a human institution but a divine creation, and that we are only instruments of God called to do God's will.

In 1973 I was called to Augustana Lutheran Church in Baltimore, Maryland. The assistant to the bishop told me to "run the church like any other business." I was young and inexperienced. His advice seemed prudent. It was also absolutely wrong. Businesses are driven by the motive of profit. It is the call of God to do ministry in a particular community that drives the church. Churches do not fail because of inability to make a profit or to balance a budget. They fail because the congregation's leaders—clergy and lay—lack vision for ministry. The writer of Proverbs puts it this way: "Where there is no vision the people perish" (Proverbs 29:18 KJV).

Vision is not wishful day dreaming, nor does it originate in the human imagination. Vision is the ability to catch a glimpse of the dreams of God. In order for that to happen, leaders in the church must be grounded in sound biblical theology and sustained by an active life of prayer.

The Congregation Council

It seems that each denomination has a different name for the board that is responsible for congregational leadership and decision making. In the Evangelical Lutheran Church in America, the official name for such a group is the "congregation council," and I will use that designation here (although most members use the older term, "church council"). In other denominations, the governing board is called the vestry, the session, or the board of elders.

The congregation council—by its actions, demeanor, and understanding of ministry—sets the tone for the congregation. It not only maintains the ongoing ministry of the church, it develops new programs, supports the pastors and the staff, and helps shape the vision of ministry for the congregation. It is an awesome task and a great responsibility. For them to be faithful and effective leaders, congregation council members need training and an understanding of what is expected from them. The following are suggestions that might help the congregation council become a body of spiritual leaders who ensure an active ministry rather than a board of directors who do only what "we can afford."

A Biblically Informed Theology of the Church

I have become convinced that one of the most important functions the pastor can have on the council is that of teacher. During most Lenten seasons, the council at Gloria Dei! ceases to have regular business meetings. Instead, we gather three, four, or five times for study and prayer. Every few years, we write a theology of the church. This becomes the basis for our mission statement. The studies have four goals:

1. Through Bible study, look at the character of the ministry of Jesus and his followers.

2. Write a brief theology of the church that grows out of the Bible study.

3. Contextualize the theology of the church for our particular ministry setting.

4. Examine our existing programs and ask, Do they reflect our theology

of the church? Are we carrying out these programs faithfully? Are they effective?

This exercise is not only instructive, it encourages council members to examine actively their faith and the call of the church to ministry.

A five-session study led by the pastor and congregation president might look like this:

Session 1: Bible Study of Mark 1-4. What was the ministry of Jesus like? What kinds of activities did Jesus do? What are some common themes in the parables of Mark 4?

Session 2: Bible Study on Selected Gospel Texts. What were Jesus' instructions for ministry? Appropriate texts include Matthew 20:25-28; 21:13-14; 25:31-46: 28:16-20; Luke 9:2; John 13:12-15; 13:31-35; 14:12; 15:12-17; 21:15-17; and others of your own choosing. It is not necessary to do detailed exegesis. Simply read each text and ask for comments about the implications for Christian ministry.Then discuss the implications of the passage for your context.

Session 3: A Theology of the Church. Based on the study, if Jesus were to write a theology of the church for your congregation, what would it look like? Take a stab at writing one. This is an extremely interesting exercise.

Session 4: A Study of Ministry. Does our ministry faithfully reflect our theology of the church? Are we effective in our ministry? Where do we need to make improvements?

Session 5: A Mission Statement. Are there programs or areas of ministry we feel called to implement or increase? Write a new mission statement of no more than one or two paragraphs that reflects the learning of the group.

Prayer and Council Meetings

Not too long ago one of our council members suggested, "We need to pray more at meetings. We need to pray for each other and for the wisdom to do God's will." She was right. It is easy for councils to get so caught up in "important business" that we neglect to pray. Everyone who comes to a council meeting brings at least three agendas. Each person brings personal concerns. He might be worried about a parent or a spouse. She might be concerned about children, her own health, or work. Even if they are not shared, these agendas will affect the council person's ability to listen and respond. Henri Nouwen once delivered a speech titled "The Church Is the Place to Share the Pain." If there is no time for personal sharing and prayer, people not only come to the meeting hurting, they leave hurting and no healing is possible. But council members can be spiritually supportive of each other even when the specific nature of the pain is not shared.

Second, people generally have their own agendas for the church. Some come wanting to increase social ministry, or add a program for children, or decrease the budget, or have more dinners. Corporate prayer is essential. In it, council members ask, Lord, what are we called to do? Congregations cannot do everything. To be effective, councils must pray constantly, "Not my will but thy will be done."

Finally, people do not serve on the council unless they are genuinely committed to the church. Most of the time people come to council meetings wanting to do what is best for the congregation. Councils need to spend some time in prayer, giving thanks for the leadership of pastors, staff, and council members,

When Gloria Dei! was considering a building program, one member suggested that each person spend the month of June in daily prayer about it. We had already planned a major capital fund campaign for that next February. At the July council meeting, each council member was asked to comment on the building program and the proposed capital fund campaign. One by one, they all said the same thing: "I am committed to the building program but we should wait until the following fall to have the capital fund drive." Prudence suggested we should not wait. But based on the collective wisdom of our members discerned through prayer, we waited.

Prayer is the most valuable asset for Christian ministry boards. It

holds them together, encourages them to love each other, depend on
God, and hold up a vision for ministry. Sometimes, however, the very
structure of council meetings mitigates against such spiritual leadership.
Meetings tend to become similar to corporate board meetings where
members ask, Where can we save money? rather than a religious gathering of faithful people who ask, How can we better serve and proclaim
God's grace? Pastor Mark Dill of St. John's Lutheran Church in
Cumberland, Maryland, uses the following "liturgy" for church council
meetings.

Liturgy for Our Church Council Meeting

• Opening Devotions
• Sharing Our Joys and Concerns
• The Litany
    • Minutes of our last meeting
    • Other communications
• Our Offerings to the Lord (giving our money, our time, and our posses-
  sions)
    • Words from committees about our ministries
• Words for Reflection (discussion on a theme or pressing congregational
  issue)
• Our History as God's People (old business)
• Our Vision and Mission for the Future (new business)
• Prayers of the People (based on joys and concerns shared and the
  pressing needs of the congregation)
• The Lord's Prayer
• Sharing God's Peace in Food and Fellowship

Structuring the work of the council as a liturgy can help remind
council members that the work of the council is indeed a spiritual under-
taking that both depends on and contributes to members' growing relationship with God. When council members are not encouraged in such
ministry, their spiritual well-being is not nurtured. And *where spirituality
diminishes, formalism and legalism thrive*. Christian history is replete
with spiritual leaders who found a movement and leave a legacy of faithful service. Often times disciples, in their eagerness to guarantee the

movement's survival, set up rules and regulations that they feel their
mentor would want. Because they lack the leader's spiritual depth, the
movement often degenerates into formal ritualistic practices that choke
the spiritual breath that had spawned the movement. Church councils that
lack loving spiritual discipline can do the same.

The Devotional Life of Individual Council Members

The congregation cannot grow in faith or love beyond that of the pastor
and church council. That may seem overstated. Nonetheless, it is true.
The church council both reflects the congregational level of spirituality
and leads by example.

Council members should daily pray for every other council person
by name. They should pray for the pastors and staff. They should keep a
church roster handy and pray for individual members each day. And they
should pray for the ability to love each other and discern God's will.
(This might seem like a lot for a council member to undertake, but can
you imagine the results in the life of the congregation?) Finally, it should
be publicized that the congregation council is a praying body and that
each member has a disciplined daily devotional life.

Administration as a Spiritual Exercise

Like the pastor, the congregation council is active in managing programs
and is concerned about the well-being of the congregation as a whole.
Among other things, its duties include staff oversight, finance, and program administration. Council members are the designated futurists, revealing the shape of tomorrow's ministry. The council provides direction
for ministry that is faithful to the Gospel and effectively implemented.
And it ensures that parts of the organizational body fit together into a
healthy and whole organism. St. Paul's illustration of the church as a
body can be the cornerstone for an administrative model. The following
rewording of St. Paul's lesson in 1 Corinthians 12:12 and 27 expresses
that sentiment: "For just as the body is one and has many member *committees and organizations,* and all the member committees and organizations, though many, are one body, so it is with Christ. Now you, *the
church,* are the body of Christ and individual members of it."

Rather than organizational flow charts that describe function, church councils, pastors, and staff would be better served by an organic diagram that describes the ontological truth of the church. The following chart is an example of what one could look like.

The center and the context of the organization is God. Pastors, lay president, and council members have a relationship with each part of the body. Each member of the body is important in its own right and in the manner in which it fits with the other members and functions in the body as a whole. The council guarantees that the congregational focus is doing God's will and maintaining the wholeness and health of the body. Turmoil and conflict in one part of the body affect the entire church body. The greatest service a congregation council can perform is to help each part of the body work together in harmony for the faithful proclamation of the Gospel and the well-being of the church. In a very real sense, the council does pastoral ministry, caring for the whole as well as the individual.

Qualifications for Congregation Council Membership

Every congregation has its own particular method of nominating and electing church council members. Some use an ecclesiastical ballot. Some have a formal nomination process. Whatever process your congregation uses, it is important to have some qualifications in mind for membership on the council. First a word of caution: Setting qualifications can be dangerous. We can become pharisaic or "holier than thou" in our assessment of people's ability to serve. Nonetheless, we make assessments regularly. In my years in ministry I have heard, among others, the following used as criteria for church council membership: "He has a good business head." "She has been a member a long time." "It might be a way of getting him more active." "She's a teacher; we need a new Christian education chair." "She really has broad administrative experience."

While some of these qualifications are important for effective service, other qualities are even more important. I know many congregations that run like well-oiled administrative machines with each part functioning in perfect symmetry with the others. Yet in a very real sense, the congregations have lost their soul. They may preach that God is the source of life and gives direction to our ministry. Their actions, however, declare success comes from human initiative and worldly wisdom. While it is risky business to judge another's heart, it is possible to ask a few pertinent questions: Is he faithful at worship? Does she participate in the

Christian education programs of the church? Does he participate in a
Bible study? Is she active in the life of the church?

Similarly, it is important to have a good mix of men and women,
people who grew up in the denomination and people who did not, long-
time members and new members, older people and young people, married
people with children and singles, and so forth. A congregation council
needs to be like the stained glass window of a church nave. Each piece of
glass has its own color, shade, shape, and place in the window. Even
though the same sun shines through the window, each piece of glass individually and distinctively reflects the rays. Yet it is how the pieces of
glass fit and work together as a whole that is important to the beauty of
the window. Membership on the congregation council is not only a matter of recruiting people with varied talents but of realizing that God needs
to be reflected in their lives.

St. Paul had some pretty stringent qualifications for the deacons of
his day. "Deacons must be serious, not double-tongued, not indulging in
much wine, not greedy for money; they must hold fast to the mystery of
the faith with a clear conscience. And let them first be tested; then if they
prove themselves blameless, let them serve as deacons" (1 Timothy
3:8-10. See also Acts 6:1-7.) Clearly, qualifications for church council
memberships need to be studied, prayed about, debated, agreed upon—
and posted.

Committees and Organizations

Earlier in this book I said that church members have big hearts and want
to serve on committees or join service organizations even at the expense
of their own spiritual nurture. I suggested that each parishioner needs one
place to serve and one place to be nurtured. It is possible to design committee and organizational functions so that they can spiritually nurture
the participants. For instance, choir practice can be more than music rehearsal. Members can worship while perfecting the art. The altar guild
can turn preparations for celebration of the Eucharist or preparing the
altar into reverent acts that bring members a sense of the presence of
God. Property committees that change air filters, work in the flower garden, or clean the kitchen can even think of their work as preparing the
church property to host a festive meeting of God and members of God's

family. Our work can become holy if we allow it and do it in the spirit of divine service. I know one congregation that has a great many committees that meet monthly. Their meetings last ninety minutes, of which forty-five are spent in Bible study and prayer.

The Spiritual Nurture Committee

Most churches do not need new committees. To be perfectly frank, I think most have too many and have them do only busy work. Nonetheless, I suggest that each congregation have one committee that has as its primary goal the spiritual nurture of the congregation. The chair should serve on the council as well.

The purpose of the spiritual nurture committee is to provide a variety of opportunities for spiritual growth to take place in the congregation. The chair should help the council keep spiritually centered and focused. Its duties would include: organizing weekend retreats; providing weekday classes on prayer and spiritual growth; organizing and publicizing prayer vigils; scheduling quiet days; providing and maintaining a "quiet room" at church; supporting the prayer chain and the mothers' prayer chain; with the clergy, designing special worship services; encouraging, supporting, or initiating the design and publication of original devotional material; providing other devotional material as needed; supporting Bible study leaders; implementing other programs as they see fit.

In summary, the spiritual nurture committee keeps the congregation focused on spiritual growth and matters of faith and prayer.

The Prayer Chain

Many congregations have some kind of prayer chain. Briefly, a prayer chain is a group or groups of individuals charged with the responsibility of intercessory prayer. Each chain has a leader who is called with a specific prayer request. The leader then calls the next person on the chain, who calls the next person, who calls the next person, and on down the line. Confidentiality is required and records should be kept by the leader. Some prayer chains send a notice or scripture readings or a note of concern to the person who is being remembered in prayer. It is very humbling and gratifying to know that one is being prayed for. Prayer chains can also pray the church roster, praying through the list of members alphabetically week by week. The members who are to be prayed for could be called and asked if they have any specific prayer requests.

Pastors need to be especially supportive of the prayer chain because, with the permission of the person being prayed for, clergy can supply additional names of people to be remembered in prayer. If confidentiality needs to be maintained, the pastor can always just give an initial. God will know who the person is even if members of the prayer chain do not.

Providing for the spiritual nurture of the congregation is more than offering a specific program or event. It is ministry that begins with the pastor and congregation council and potentially includes every member. It is ministry that takes prayer, vision, and perseverance.

CHAPTER 12

The Pastor

This morning I prayed hard for my parish, my poor parish, my first and perhaps my last, since I ask no better than to die here. My parish! The words can't even be spoken without a kind of soaring love.

—George Bernanos, *Diary of a Country Priest*

The Birthing of a Pastor

The year 1968 was momentous in American history: Martin Luther King Jr. had been assassinated in Memphis; Bobby Kennedy was fatally shot in Los Angeles; cities and college campuses endured constant tension; racial unrest was widespread; and the Vietnam War divided the nation. In the midst of this political turmoil and social unrest, I entered seminary. Like many others, I had heard the call to the ministry and, like many others, I had little appreciation of its significance. One of my professors was the saintly Dr. Edmund Smits, a Latvian refugee. I registered for his classes not because of the subject matter but simply to be in his presence. One day my classmates and I were participating in one of our favorite pseudointellectual pastimes—"fundy bashing." Dr. Smits would have none of it. He simply replied, "Fundamentalists died better in the concentration camp. Faith is more important than theological acumen." I promptly filed his comment under interesting but useless information. I was too busy becoming a systematic theologian, biblical exegete, and social reformer to worry about what that statement meant.

My dad preached at my ordination in 1972. His text was an appropriate ordination text: John 21:15-19 ("If you love me feed my sheep").

During the course of the sermon, Dad made a special point to tell me to
eat before I feed—to feast on the word of God before I offer the bread of
life. Because I loved and respected my father I listened attentively, but in
my heart knew that I did not have time to eat. I was going to feed the
world, change the world—indeed, save the world. Racial tensions were
still high, cities needed to be revitalized, and the Vietnam War was still
being fought. There was too much to accomplish to spend much time
eating spiritual food. I was a city pastor struggling to make a difference
in people's lives. Work consumed me. I slept at church at least two
nights a week, started smoking, and gained thirty pounds. (I was not too
busy to feast on a good Big Mac!) The inevitable happened. My life
became cold and joyless. My sermons lacked spiritual depth and insight.
My six-year-old daughter at one point said to me, "We're not a family
anymore. You never even eat at home." Finally, a friend of mine confronted me with my own folly. "Tell me, Tom," he began, "what do you
tell people who want to become members of your church? Join and you
can become just like me—an overweight smoker, filled with self-pity
who is neglecting his family? Paul said, 'Glorify God in your body.' To
whom does your life and body give glory? I'm going to change your
life!" And change it he did. That moment was my Damascus Road experience. All at once, everything people had been expressing to me about
growing spiritually and caring for myself physically, emotionally, and
socially made sense.

My mentor, Father William from Holy Cross Abbey, challenged me
by saying, "The congregation as a whole cannot grow in faith beyond
that of the pastor. Individuals can, but not the congregation as a whole."
Dom Ambrose of Bolton Abbey in Ireland simply said, "We must lead
by example." His words seem obvious, but they convey a deep and
sometimes forgotten truth.

This chapter is not about creating guilt or adding one more burden to
the long list of "essential pastoral tasks." It is a gentle reminder of truths
you already know:

1. You must dine at the table of our Lord's presence before you feed the
   Lord's sheep.

2. You need to provide your people a healthy and human example of
   Christian living. Ordination does not impose the condition of holiness,
   but it does demand that we call upon the Holy one to lead us.

"But as for you, man of God, shun all this; pursue righteousness, godliness, faith, love, endurance, gentleness. Fight the good fight of the faith; take hold of the eternal life, to which you were called and for which you made the good confession in the presence of many witnesses" (1 Timothy 6:11-12).

The Devotional Life of the Pastor

Who is more privileged than the parish pastor? We proclaim the loving acceptance of God when a child is baptized. We preside at the weddings of people we cherish. We are asked to venture into the secret hidden caverns of people's hearts with the light of God's presence. We proclaim the hope of resurrection at the bedside of the dying and, at the cemetery, to the grieving. Pastors are simply lovers of God's people. How many times have you called someone on an impulse only to hear, "Pastor, I'm so glad you called. I so wanted to talk to you"? We touch life at its core. In order to do the job effectively, pastors need to be clothed with the Word of God. An ancient anonymous writer put it this way: "One who preaches God's word and is not comforted, strengthened, rebuked, and humbled by it is like a man who sits by a spring and goes thirsty, who had bread in his hands and goes hungry."

The pastor's first and foremost responsibility is to know and love God. Devotional immersion in the Bible and fidelity in prayer are the tools we use to build that relationship of intimate knowledge and abiding love. Reading the Bible devotionally is sometimes difficult for clergy. We are trained to do exegesis. An Episcopal priest once told me, "There are two naivetes in reading the Bible. The first comes in seminary where we learn form criticism and literary criticism. We hear about *heilsgeschichte* and Rudolf Bultmann. The second naivete comes later when we discover that God can speak to us through Scripture without the higher biblical critical methods."

An old pastor gave me his Bible when he retired. It had been his prayer book during a lifetime of ministry. It was worn. The pages no longer stayed in the binding. It was underlined, stuffed with little papers, and the margins were filled with personal notes written as he read and prayed. While exegesis is important for study and sermon preparations, reading the Bible as God's Word to us in the midst of our busy lives is essential.

So is reading extrabiblical material. There is a whole body of
Christian literature that often remains untaught in seminary: mystical
theology and spiritual literature. There are a host of great spiritual writings that often are not read in Protestant seminaries. They include writings of the Desert Fathers and Mothers, the *Conferences* of John Cassian,
Augustine's *Confessions,* St. Bernard's *Sermons on the Song of Songs,*
The Little Flowers of St. Francis, Interior Castle by St. Teresa, *Showings*
by Julian of Norwich, and *The Cloud of Unknowing.* There are also many
great spiritual writers in your theological tradition that go unread. These
writings connect us with the giants of the faith, and their words, ideas,
and lives can inspire us to expand our understanding of God.

The Pastor as Intercessor

Shortly after I was ordained, I called my dad and complained about my
parishioners. He stopped me in midsentence and asserted as only a father
can, "Please don't complain to me about your congregation. Don't complain about them in public either. Don't even complain about them to
God. You were not called to complain about them, but to pray for them,
love them, proclaim God's word, administer the sacraments, and lead
them in a Godly way." He was not saying, "Don't discuss problems you
are having" but "Don't berate people in public." Quite often I hear clergy
speak in a very derogatory way about their people. Maybe part of the
problem should rest at the pastor's doorstep. We clergy often fail to remember our people in prayer.

St. Paul addressed the issue: "... without ceasing I remember you
always in my prayers," he writes to the church at Rome (Romans 1:9).
Even in Paul's second letter to Corinth, when the relationship between
Paul and the Corinthians' church had deteriorated—and the pain was
evident—he wrote as a pastor who loved his church and prayed for his
people.

The pastor, as a regular part of devotions, should pray for each
member individually, even if prayer is offered for only five people a day.
We can visualize the members' homes, life settings, and faces, and pray
for their special needs. Pray for the gifts of the Holy Spirit, for church
leaders, and for all clergy. Pray for the "thorns in the side." Someone
once said, "Friends come and go, but enemies accumulate." The best way

to change that scenario is to "pray for those who persecute you." Inter-cessory prayer for the church and for our members is an obligation both of our calling and the exhortation of love.

Prayer helps us become better preachers and worship leaders. I can always tell when I am not spiritually prepared to lead worship. I might try to hide it, but my demeanor exposes me to those who know me best. When we preach we use two voices: a human voice and a divine voice. On the one hand, the message must clearly reflect understanding of the human condition. The preacher needs to comprehend the pain of life as well as the joy of living. On the other hand, the congregation wants more than human commiserating. They ask, "Is there any word from the Lord?" The divine voice is the message of God to the people of God. We hear it through study, reflection, and prayer. We declare it by grace.

For Further Reading

Doberstein, John W. *Minister's Prayer Book.* Philadelphia: Muhlenberg Press, n.d.

CHAPTER 13

The Pastor as Spiritual Guide

The Counseling Pastor

The pastor's study is a safe harbor for those who find themselves foundering in troubled waters. Few professionals have greater access to the lives of people than the parish pastor. Parishioners open the doors to their heart and say, "Enter gently." They come for a variety of reasons. Some come because the pastor is a trusted and respected member of the community. Some come because they have an ongoing relationship with the pastor. Others come because it is the only port in a storm. They bring a medley of problems: depression, grief, marital discord, child problems, parent problems, drug and alcohol addictions, and more. They come with issues great and small. One thing is certain: They will come.

Much of the time the pastor will know the parishioner rather well. The pastor might have baptized a baby, officiated at a child's wedding, or sat beside the counselee at a potluck supper. Clergy, unlike others in the helping professions, usually know their people formally and informally. The parishioner knows something about the pastor, as well, about family, hobbies, flaws, and so on. They also know the pastor is a person of God. They come to present a problem or a crisis, or merely to seek advice. They also come needing and wanting to find God's presence. They come hungry for God.

Sometimes, for a variety of reasons, we clergy forget how important this hunger is. Periodically, we might neglect to pray with the people who come to us. People long to see the finger of God touching their lives. Clergy can help them sit still long enough to allow God to catch them. Clergy can help them pray. Quite often I will place an empty chair in our midst as a reminder of our unseen participant. Besides dealing with problems, clergy can help the person understand that God is present, active, and trustworthy in his life.

To be a pastoral counselor is in fact to be a spiritual guide helping people find their way in life's dark maze. This can be accomplished through discussion, scripture readxing, and prayer. It can also be aided by guided meditation. Meditation is intended to help create a spiritual atmosphere in which a person can feel God's presence. Logic seldom convinces someone of a spiritual truth as deeply as an experience of God's presence and healing touch.

Following are two simple examples of guided meditation to assist the pastor in this endeavor. I was taught the method by the Rev. Tilden Edwards of the Shalem Institute.[1] Tilden learned them from someone else.

Guided Meditation

A. Preliminary issues

1. Explain that the meditation is simply a method to help a person feel aware of God's presence. It might work, and it might not. Try not to judge it. Just allow the experience to unfold naturally.

2. Give the counselee freedom either to share about the experience or to keep the experience private.

3. Help the person find a chair that will allow her to sit with her back straight, with both feet flat on the floor, and to sit comfortably with her hands in her lap.

4. Tell the counselee that you are going to read a text from Scripture, read it a second time, and then place her in the scene and retell the story again. Explain that there will be a period of silence and that you will end the silence by saying the Lord's Prayer together.

B. A meditation that can be used with almost anyone, including in a class or small group setting

1. Read Mark 10:46-52 to familiarize the counselee with the text.

2. Help her get settled and comfortable. Ask her to close her eyes, thereby shutting out at least half of the inevitable distractions.

3. Reread the text slowly, pausing at what seem to be appropriate places.

4. Tell the story in your own words and place her in the text. What follows is a sample of what I do. Do whatever seems to fit your style and personality best.

It is sunrise. You are standing on a hillside leaning against a lone tree just off the road to Jericho. It is a glorious morning, cool and still. The sun is just peeking out above the rooftops of that great walled city. Across the road from you and about fifty yards toward the town sits a blind man—Bartimaeus. As you watch the sun continue to rise, you notice a group of people coming out of the city toward you. The road is dry, and the crowd kicks up dust as it approaches. All of a sudden the cry of Bartimaeus stops the crowd: "Jesus, Son of David, have mercy on me!" Some in the crowd order him to be silent with stern words: "Who are you to be calling on the Master? Be still!" But Bartimaeus is undeterred and cries out all the louder, "Jesus, Son of David, have mercy on me!" You feel empathy for the poor man in his need. And Jesus stands still. "Bring him to me," Jesus says. Immediately someone goes to the beggar and explains, "Take heart, Jesus is calling you." The blind man throws off his coat, springs to his feet, and is led to Jesus. Jesus looks at Bartimaeus. It is a look of love. As Jesus places his hand on the man's shoulder he says, "What do you want me to do for you?" "Oh, Master," Bartimaeus answers, "let me receive my sight." In a voice filled with authority Jesus declares, "Go, your faith has made you whole." The man sees. You are amazed because never have you seen such a thing. Bartimaeus thanks Jesus and dashes off toward town to tell his family and friends of this great event. The people in the crowd, speaking to each about this miracle, slowly begin to wander back to town. You continue to stand under that tree and watch them leave. The disciples continue their journey and walk away from town. But Jesus hasn't moved. The crowd is now gone, leaving only a trace of dust in the air. The disciples disappear over a hill. Jesus turns and looks in your direction. "What do you want me to do for you?" Jesus asked with hands outstretched. "Oh, Master," you answer, "let me receive my sight."

You and the Master are alone.

5. Allow the counselee to stay in silence for at least ten minutes. It might take her a while to get into it. She might have to get past thinking, "This is stupid!" or "What am I supposed to do?" She might fidget. It is okay. Pray for the counselee at this time, silently. Pray that God gives her the sight she needs. Try to be still so the counselee might draw inspiration from your silence.

6. Say the Lord's Prayer out loud and very slowly. She might or might not join in.

7. Open your eyes. Say nothing for a minute or so. Allow the moment to help you decide what to do next. Talking about the experience is not always helpful. Suggest that she go back to that Jericho road once a day for the next week or until she comes back to see you.

C. A meditation to be used when a person feels guilty

A psychiatrist once said to me, "Most of my patients would be better off in your office. They need to feel forgiven." A great gift of the church is the order of confession and forgiveness. Periodically that is all an individual needs. Sometimes people feel forgiven all at once. I think, however, that for most a feeling of being forgiven grows slowly and over the course of time. It is more authoritative if parishioners can hear words of forgiveness from our Lord rather than from us. I have used the following guided meditation for many years and have found it to be a very helpful supplement to the order of private confession.

1. I introduce the text, John 8:2-11. I almost always tell people that many scholars do not think this text was in John's original manuscript, but that the incident was authentic and inserted later. Depending on the person, this explanation may take a few minutes. The reason I bring it up is that some editions of the Bible include this text only as a footnote. Read the text.

2. Follow the same procedure as in section A above to ready the counselee. A brief discussion about forgiveness is also helpful in preparing for this meditation. Use plenty of biblical texts in the discussion.

3. Reread the text after the person is quiet and has settled down with his eyes closed. Allow a few minutes for silence. Next, tell the story in your own words. The following is a sample of what I do. It is important not to rush the story. Do not be afraid of pauses.

It is early in the morning. The sun isn't even visible. There is just the glow of predawn. You are in the courtyard of the temple praying. *(Pause.)* The temple is a massive building, but you find a private quiet corner. *(Pause.)* You hear a noise and notice a man enter. It is Jesus. A dozen or so people are following him. "Master, teach us," they implore. Jesus sits down on the ground a few yards from you and begins to speak. "Come to me, you who are weary. I will give you rest." *(Pause.)* "I came that you might have life and have it abundantly." *(Pause.)* "I am the good shepherd. The good shepherd lays down his life for the sheep." You hang on every word. They are food for the hungry heart. *(Pause a minute or so.)*

All of a sudden there is a commotion. Angry voices ring out: "Harlot!" "Law breaker!" The leaders in the temple are pushing their way toward Jesus. They have a woman with them. You look into her face. You see fear and embarrassment, guilt and shame. She is nearly naked, covered only with a bed sheet wrapped tightly about her. She is disheveled as they throw her at the feet of Jesus. She lands in a huddled heap. A thundering voice echoes, "This woman was caught in the very act of committing adultery. The law of Moses told us to stone such women to death. What do you say?" Jesus is silent. He says nothing. Slowly he bends down and writes on the ground with his finger. He knows their intentions. His demeanor calms them momentarily. They ask again, "Teacher, what do you say?" Jesus stands up and looks into each person's eyes. He peers into their hearts and declares, "Whoever has not sinned—you throw the first stone." You gaze at the Pharisees standing there with large stones clenched in their hands. *Thud. Thud.* The stones fall to the ground. *Thud. Thud.* One by one they fall, and one by one the accusers sneak away into the shadows.

Jesus now gazes at this woman—this guilty woman. "Woman, where are those who accused you? Has no one condemned you?" "No one, sir," she answers. "Neither do I condemn you. Go your way and leave your life of sin." The woman, standing more erect, leaves forgiven—changed, whole. Jesus then spies you over in the corner. He peers into your eyes, looks into your heart. He sees your pain. Knows your guilt. Feels your shame.

"Master," you blurt out, "help me. Forgive me. Gather me into your love."

And you and the Master are alone.

4. It is not unusual for the counselee to weep. He may in fact sob. Stay put, unless it never ends. The tears will be cleansing. There might also be unearthly sounding groans. Do not panic. Let them come. It is easy to short-circuit the healing touch of Jesus. On the other hand, nothing might happen. As above, allow at least ten minutes of silence.

5. Say the words of absolution and begin the Lord's Prayer—slowly.

6. Discussion is very appropriate at this time. Suggest the counselee "visit the temple" each day until you meet again. Remind him that sometimes feelings of complete forgiveness come slowly. Assure him that God does not want him to hold on to his guilt.

"Lord, it's dark in here. Where are You? I can't find You."

How long, O Lord? Will you forget me forever?
How long will you hide your face from me?
How long must I bear pain in my soul,
and have sorrow in my heart all day long?

(Psalm 13:1-2b)

Words similar to those have been uttered in most pastors' studies. Sometimes people feel they are praying to a stone God. They are experiencing a spiritually dry time. The mystics called it "the dark night." It could be they are experiencing what Luther called the "Deus Absconditus" or the "hidden God." A parishioner might come and quietly confide, "Pastor, I'm having a little problem. My faith isn't what it used to be. I can't pray. When I do pray, I don't feel God is listening. Have I lost my faith?" Sometimes he is depressed and needs to be referred. Often he might appear depressed but have a true spiritual problem. Either way, it is helpful for the pastor to see that person regularly. If you have been in the ministry for a while, you have probably developed your own methods to help people with such struggles. But here are a few additional thoughts on the subject.

1. When speaking about dry times or wilderness experiences, Thomas Merton in his book *Thoughts in Solitude* shares this insight. He begins with a discussion about the exodus and the Hebrews wandering in the desert for forty years. He explains that they could have gotten to the promised land in a few short months if they had taken a direct route. Yet they wandered, grumbling as they went, for four decades. "Why?" Merton wonders. He writes in reply, "God wanted them to love him in the desert before they loved him in the Promised Land."[2] Boris Pasternak said it this way: "You have to pay the price for living on your own naked spiritual resources." Pasternak, Soviet author of *Dr. Zhivago*, had become a Christian on his own. Someone had given him a New Testament, which he had read and studied in solitude.

In most Western countries, people's faith is propped up and sustained in community. We are taught about God at the feet of wise and loving parents, teachers, and pastors. There comes a time in many Christians' lives when those props fail to hold them up. Scripture is meaningless. Sermons fail to inspire. And God seems distant. Some Christians leave the church. Others might wander in this dark night for years. People who are experiencing a faith crisis need a guide to lead them through the desert into a promised land of a more mature faith. The price for living on one's own "naked spiritual resources" is the experience of the desert.

It might be helpful to read to a person experiencing the dark night selected sections from Exodus. Read about manna in the wilderness, quail in the evening, and water from a rock. Assure the person that God is indeed with us, even when we cannot discern it. It was during those forty years that God transformed the loosely bound Hebrew children into the nation of Israel. In the spiritual desert, God is calling the wanderer to a deeper and more mature faith. God sometimes leads people into a desert to prepare them for a more intimate knowledge and deeper relationship. In the moment, he will hate the desert, the dark night, or the experience of the hidden God. Assure the wanderer that you will walk with him or her as guide.

The following books about the dark night might be helpful:

Charles Cummings, OSCO *Spirituality and the Desert Experience*
St. John of the Cross   *The Dark Night of the Soul*
                          (various editions)
Barbara Pent   *My Only Friend is Darkness*

2. Use the psalms with him. The psalmists were very graphic about their feelings of being deserted by God. Jesus even felt a dark moment on the cross and quoted a psalm: "My God, My God, why have you forsaken me?" (Psalm 22:1). The personal laments work very well. Try selected sections from Psalms 10, 13, 22, 40, 42, 86, 88. Give the counselee homework, asking him to read them out loud or write his own psalm.

3. If he cannot pray, let him off the hook and give him permission to stop praying for a while. Give him some psalms to read. Keep in touch by phone every other day or so. He might not need much time on the phone, but a brief encounter can be very helpful.

4. Help him not to try to rush into the promised land but to wait until God leads him.

5. Remember that this can be some of the pastor's most frustrating work because we do not like to see people struggle in the faith. Patience is a virtue.

The Pastor's Pastor

Every pastor needs a special spiritual friend, someone to talk to about spiritual matters. It can be another clergy person or a lay person. I had a spiritual friend who was a dynamic and strong lay woman. We met once a month to discuss my prayer life. We did not talk about church or family, only prayer. By the same token, we also need mentors, people who can help us grow professionally. I am lucky to have had three or four in my lifetime, including my father. We all need a wise and experienced person to speak with periodically. We all need to hear the "accumulated wisdom" of the ages they can pass down to us and through us to others.

For Further Reading

May, Gerald G. *Care of Mind/Care of Spirit: A Psychiatrist Explores Spiritual Direction.* Harper: San Francisco, 1992.

_____. *Will and Spirit: A Contemplative Psychology.* San Francisco: Harper & Row, 1982.

CHAPTER 14

Spiritual Friendships

What is a spiritual friend?

After Constantine's conversion to Christianity in 312, few Christians suffered a martyr's death. Instead, men and women chose to become living martyrs for the faith and fled to the Egyptian and Syrian deserts. These Desert Fathers and Mothers lived as hermits. Their lives were austere; they fasted regularly, slept very little, and did battle with the powers of evil. Their holiness became renowned. Consequently, Christians from nearby towns and villages would seek them out to ask questions on matters of faith. Their wisdom is recorded in the *Apophthegmata Patrum* or "Sayings of the Fathers" and in the *Conferences* of John Cassian. They make fascinating reading and give many spiritual thoughts to ponder. These men and women began the ministry of spiritual direction. It flourished for centuries and reached its height in the Middle Ages.

Today spiritual direction is practically nonexistent in the Protestant church, and in the Catholic church it is practiced almost exclusively in the monastic system. Recently, however, there has been renewed interest in the tradition. Instinctively, religious people understand that they need someone to speak with about spiritual matters. Trained spiritual directors are hard to find. Consequently, a revised paradigm has emerged, that of spiritual partners or spiritual friends. People have enjoyed informal spiritual friendships for centuries. Many are now choosing to make the relationship a little more formal. Yet the concept remains simple.

A spiritual friend is a person who agrees to discuss spiritual matters with another. The relationship might be mutual or one-sided. A spiritual friend helps a person be disciplined in prayer and supports the person on his or her spiritual journey. I summarize the concept this way: *A spiritual friend agrees to speak with another at regular intervals about prayer and the presence of God in his or her life.*

The spiritual friend does not necessarily need any formal theological training. The purpose is not to discuss theology but simply to help another talk about his or her prayer life and discern God's presence in the midst of real-life situations. The spiritual friend does not need to talk as much as to keep the conversation focused on God and prayer. Because the spiritual life is not a separate compartment but encompasses all of life, discussions will cover relationships, work, and so forth. Nonetheless, the point of concentration is always on God's presence in these situations. This does not mean that problems or strained relationships are not important to talk about in their own right. It simply means that spiritual friendship is not the forum for that discussion to take place.

I have yet to hear from a parishioner, "Pastor Tom, I just wanted you to know that I am fully mature in the faith. I don't need to grow anymore." Every Christian knows that growth in faith continues throughout the course of life. Still, people's growth can be stunted or stopped. A spiritual friend helps encourage growth in the faith. Speaking with a spiritual friend reminds us that God is present, even when we cannot discern that presence. This special friend can listen to our thoughts about God and give thoughtful responses. And a spiritual companion can help a person be disciplined in the practice of prayer.

Choosing a Spiritual Friend

There are two issues involved with guiding people in their spiritual friendship. The first is helping people see the value of a spiritual friend. The second is helping people to find the right person.

The concept of spiritual friendship might be new to many people. It might be one of those ideas we need to plant like a seed in someone and allow to germinate for months and years before a sprig comes from it. Generally, people understand and can even agree with the need to talk about spiritual issues. That does not mean it will happen. Religion in the United States has become such a private and personal affair that people are reticent to discuss it, even with a close friend. Talking about faith can be very threatening. People need gentle but persistent encouragement.

Finding the right person can also be difficult. I remember hearing that individuals need two kinds of people to support them: sandpaper and blankets. The blanket kind of supporter is a person who will hold you in his or her arms and assure you that everything will be okay. Sandpaper support is like a "Dutch Uncle" saying, "Quit feeling sorry for yourself; get up and do something." It is best if spiritual friends can do both. But above all else, they should be grounded in the faith and at least as spiritually mature as the person they are befriending. It is important that they be good listeners and have the ability to be nonjudgmental on most occasions. People need a safe and nonthreatening environment in which to express their opinions and problems. The friend should also be reliable and discreet.

It might seem that helping people agree to the concept, motivating them to act, and guiding them in finding a spiritual friend might be at best difficult and at worst impossible. That is almost true. Very few people will avail themselves of this kind of relationship. The ones who do, however, will benefit greatly.

For Further Reading

Edwards, Tilden. *Spiritual Friend: Reclaiming the Gift of Spiritual Direction*. New York: Paulist Press, 1980.

PART 4

The Gifts of the Spiritual Life

CHAPTER 15

Interior Growth–Exterior Fruit

The Church's Gift to the World

In the 1930s, a family sent their sixteen-year-old son to an Oregon lumber camp to work for the summer because they were in financial need. The mother worried about how her young son would fare in the rough and tumble world of lumberjacks. Lumber camps had a reputation for being tough places with loose morals. Before the boy left, his mother lectured him, "Son, don't let those men in the lumber camp lead you astray. And be prepared; they might tease you because you are a Christian."

The young lad left and after a short time he wrote home, "I'm doing fine and, Mom, I've been here two weeks and no one has teased me yet. In fact, nobody even knows that I am a Christian!"

I am not sure that story is true, but it certainly rings true. There are many Christians who hide their faith well. Now, I am not suggesting people wear T-shirts that say "Christian." I am suggesting that being a Christian has definite implications for how one works and participates in the life of the world. In the Sermon on the Mount, Jesus declares, "Every good tree bears good fruit, but the bad tree bears bad fruit.... You will know them by their fruits" (Matthew 7:1, 7, 20). So it is with the Christian. The interior spiritual growth of the individual bears fruit in love and holiness as they are expressed in good works.

Part of the theological heritage Luther left Protestantism is the doctrine of the priesthood of all believers. All people, lay and clergy alike, are called to sacred service. All are called to be disciples. All are called to bear fruit in the world. In a very real sense, all work, if it is done to the glory of God, is holy work. All of us, in Luther's words, are called to be "little Christs" for each other. Spiritual growth is not just for self-betterment. Neither is spiritual growth only for the professional in the church. Spiritual growth must bear fruit in the life of every Christian, especially lay people, because they carry out the ministry of the church to the world. They are the ones who work in education, government, and business. Lay ministry is carried out in people's chosen vocation in the marketplace.

Lay woman Verna Dozier writes, "Lay people have power. They have power in the secular world. The lay person's primary function is out there in the world. There is a problem when the church becomes the primary focus of their lives."[1] Too often church leaders think that lay ministry is done in the church. In reality it is done in the world.

The church's gifts to the world are spiritually alive lay people empowered to live out their faith active in love where they live and work. All the programs, ideas, and theological reflections in this book address the matter of creating vital congregations who build up the laos for ministry in the world. But to grow in the Christian faith means more than growing in knowledge. The closer we are to the heart of God, the more we long to make a difference to the heart of the world. Jesus said it best in the Upper Room before he was arrested: "I give you a new commandment, that you love one another. Just as I have loved you, you also should love one another. By this everyone will know that you are my disciples, if you have love for one another" (John 13:34-35).

We humans cannot love, by the strength of our own will, as Jesus loved. That ability is the gift of grace and the result of growing deeper in faith and love toward God. Our devotional time gives God the space and time to transform us and increase our ability to love. The church's primary task is to equip the saints for service in God's creation, not to make itself stronger, bigger, or more financially sound. Those things are important, but we in the church tend to give them too high a priority. Too much Christian ministry is turned in on itself.

Someone once said to me, "The church is not a picture gallery of saints but a training camp for wobbly recruits." Spiritual enrichment prepares people for a life of Christlike love in their places of employment, at home with their families, and in the communities where they live. The English spiritual writer William Law (1686-1761) wrote in his long and ponderous book, *A Serious Call to a Devout and Holy Life*, about the same issue. He asserts that the problem with Christianity is not that Christians resemble nonbelievers in their faults. That is understand-able. We are all human. The problem is that nonbelievers resemble Christians in their chief traits. We fail to love as Jesus loved, not because the effort is lacking, but because we try to do it of our own strength. Law goes on to say that Christianity is judged by its fruits, not by its religious observances. What goes on inside a person is important. What comes out of a person is more important.

In a Christmas sermon, Meister Eckhart (c.1260-c.1329) declared that to be a Christian is to give birth. He said in good medieval symbol-ism that the Christian undergoes three births: our own physical birth, God birthed in us, and our birth as sons and daughters of God. Out of this union with God, we give birth to love, the way Jesus loved. That ability comes only as we are in relationship to God.[2]

The better churches feed; educate; foster love for God, others, and self; and inspire members for service, the more the world will benefit from Christianity. The world requires people of integrity who appreciate the created dignity in others. Business is desperate for honest men and women who treat each other fairly. Good government demands that Christian people work for peace, justice, and equity. These wobbly re-cruits are sitting in our pews waiting to become trained disciples. I can think of no better place for this training to take place than in the Body of Christ as they assemble in communities of faith.

An In-Life Retreat

Every day Christians are confronted by a collision of values. Cheating, dishonesty, self-serving policies, outrageous profit making, and the like, are deemed prudent, in our best interests, or good business. At times this troubles Christian men and women. At other times, they do not even no-tice the clash of values. The following tool was devised by Jack Schell, a layman in my parish and an executive with the Department of the Navy in Washington, D.C. Its purpose is twofold:

(1) to afford people the opportunity of a spiritual retreat when it is impossible to get away;

(2) to bring deliberately to places of employment the values of the Christian faith and struggle with them there.

A. An Overview

Seldom do we have the occasion to participate in extended retreats away from our daily responsibilities. The in-life retreat is a means of seeking spiritual refuge while living in our everyday situations. It begins with the individual making an explicit decision to seek out greater intimacy with God for a defined period. The period should have an expressed starting point and specific end point to distinctly separate it from regular days. A period of a week, two weeks, a month, or forty days are reasonable time frames to consider for in-life retreats. We would like to suggest as a beginning that you make an in-life retreat during Holy Week.

B. The Purpose

The purpose of the in-life retreat is not only to restore our souls, minds, bodies, and hearts but to open our eyes to grasp more fully the contrast between God's holy message and our ways in the world. The main objective is to follow God's Word more intentionally and experience its depth more fully.

The Holy Week in-life retreat can help bring us to greater spiritual awareness. It is a virtual detachment for a while from the world's busyness and confusion to attain spiritual renewal. It includes becoming more open to inviting God into our lives, building on our spiritual strengths, sensing a spiritual call, and deepening our understanding of faith itself.

C. Guidelines

The three basic guidelines for an in-life retreat are intended to guide us to spiritual *simplicity*. The approach is to separate ourselves from distractions and to practice "uncomplicating" our lives.

1. Seek simplicity in relationships.

   • Seek God through silence; dramatically increase the amount of listen
   ing. This purpose of this listening is not to judge, to learn, or to feel
   superior, but to be aware of that which is invisible.
   • Spend time listening for the good.

• Place much of our passion, emotion, and worry in God's hands.
• Be hospitable. Graciously accept what people do for you.

2. Seek simplicity in goodness.

• Go out of your way to avoid controversies.
• Be less conspicuous.
• Desire awareness of God over desire of things.
• Discern temptation when it comes and seek God's help to resist.
• Perform acts of charity without regard to acknowledgments.
• Become a quiet witness of God's Word.
• Give thanks for the simple things of life.
• Seek simplicity in thought. Seek new ideas or correct ills another week.
• Be intentional about keeping a less hurried pace.

3. Seek simplicity in learning.

• Read only Scripture.
• Seek spiritual awareness instead of earthly knowledge, or philosophical or political speculation.
• Strive for a quiet mind.
• Try not to measure your spiritual growth.
• Stand in awe at the majesty of God's creation.
• Begin and end each day with prayer and scripture reading.

D. Some Tips

1. This is not easy. It takes discipline. But be gentle with yourself. The goal is not perfection but greater awareness of God and a deepening of joy, peace, and love.

2. Make prayer central to the retreat. Try to use the "simplest" prayers. Pray in uncomplicated ways, as Jesus taught us. Slowly say the "Our Father." Also use prayers from the psalter, for instance, the Twenty-Third Psalm.

3. Keep a short journal to record any changes in perspective or areas for follow-up after the retreat is completed.

4. Think about what spiritual gifts or leanings from the week you can bring to your life outside retreat time.

The Gift to the Church

Congregations benefit greatly when members are nurtured spiritually. Members' service to the church is more profound and generally more willing. Members burn out less often because they are well fed. The spirit of the church is more uplifting when members are afforded the opportunity to focus on God. Members may experience a sense of freedom and relief when they realize that their first objective is to grow in faith through participation in one or more of the available groups, programs, classes, or worship. They all want to grow but feel that first they must serve. I have had many join the church and apologetically say, "Pastor, if it is okay with you, we'd like to sit back for a while before we get involved on a committee. We got burned out in our last church." Relief leaps across their faces when I tell them that I do not want them to serve on a committee until they have been spiritually nurtured, and that this congregation is here to undergird them and help them grow closer to God.

Spiritually alive and active members bring ideas and leadership. The mother's prayer chain, quiet day, women's retreats, men's breakfasts, the book study group, and the in-life retreat are all ideas that grew out of Gloria Dei! They were not programs I began but gifts to the church from members of the church.

Additionally, I am convinced that a congregation that has great spiritual depth has a greater opportunity for internal harmony. A former bishop said to me, "Our congregations are in crisis. Only one-third of our congregations are healthy, meaning the people and pastor get along with each other. About one-third are squeaking by and tolerate each other. The other third are in civil war." I am not sure statistics bear out his one-third theory. Nonetheless, many congregations are in turmoil. The reasons are many and varied. The church has experienced controversy since the beginning, when James and John asked to sit at the right and left hand of Jesus. It has dealt with theological disputes as far back as Saints Peter and Paul. As long as there are humans, there will be power struggles and ideological differences. Much of the trouble, however, can be

either averted or minimized when clergy, staff, lay leaders, and the congregation seek first to love God and discern God's will, and second seek
to serve God in loving service. A church that is spiritually alive through
prayer, study, and vibrant worship is less likely to suffer the long-term
affects of major controversies. Where spirituality diminishes, legalism
and formalism thrive. Both are enemies of harmony and effective ministry.

A church that is spiritually alive is a gift to the entire body of Christ
and a gift in and of itself. The gift is simply an educated and faithful
laity. That may be the greatest gift the church can give.

CHAPTER 16

The Fruits of Prayer

The Gift of Yourself

We humans are greater than the sum of our physical parts. We are more than progenies of our parents. We are God's beloved children, formed and fashioned by the hands of the creator. Each of us is a gift. In God we discover those gifts and what they mean in our lives. We comprehend our place in the world and appreciate our own intrinsic worth. The psalmist jubilantly proclaims, "You have made [human beings] a little lower than God and crowned them with glory and honor" (Psalm 8:5). Irenaeus said, "The glory of God is a human fully alive."

One of the fruits of a prayerful life is the discovery of the dignity in which the psalmist exulted. The discovery of that dignity is to become fully alive in Christ

Each person is born with a unique combination of talents and desires, strengths and weaknesses, likes and dislikes, and a distinct personality. Each child of God is unique in the history of the world. Each person is to be cherished and treasured. God knows each of us intimately. Indeed, God is nearer to us than we are to ourselves. In awe and wonder the psalmist wrote:

> For it was you who formed my inward parts;
> > you knit me together in my mother's womb.
> I praise you, for I am fearfully and wonderfully made.
> > Wonderful are your works;
> that I know very well.
> > My frame was not hidden from you,

when I was being made in secret,
    intricately woven in the depths of the earth.
Your eyes beheld my unformed substance.
In all your book were written
    all the days that were formed for me,
    when none of them as yet existed.
                              (Psalm 139:13-16)

The gift of prayer and silent listening is intimacy with God. The gift of God is who I am. The gift of intimacy with God is the ability to catch a glimpse of my true identity, discover my place in the world, and discern my life's meaning and purpose. We cannot make those discoveries outside a relationship with God. "God alone possesses the secret of my identity, [God] alone can make me ... who I will be when at last I fully begin to be."[1]

God fashioned each person with a purpose. We all have a special place in the world and in the body of Christ, the church. All of us, lay and clergy, have a calling. Hearing the call brings joy. Responding to the call brings peace. Obeying the call gives our lives meaning. Churches that foster spiritual growth through prayer, study, worship, and service afford people the opportunity to appreciate the gift of who they are and discover their place in the world.

An ancient tale[2] tells of an aimless young man, Abraheem, hunting in the Egyptian desert. He was on horseback with his dog at his side. As he was riding, a voice reverberated around him: "Abraheem, Abraheem it was not for this that you were created. It was not this you were meant to do." Abraheem paused for a moment and looked around. Seeing no one, he continued on his way.

A second time he heard the voice: "Abraheem, Abraheem it was not for this that you were created. It was not this you were meant to do." Again he stopped, looked around, and seeing no one spurred his horse, called his dog, and sped off.

A third time a voice resounded. This time it came from the bowl of his saddle. "Abraheem, Abraheem it as not for this that you were created. It was not this you were meant to do." This time he dismounted, knelt down, and simply said, "You have roused me, Lord." In good, ancient Egyptian fashion, he went out into the desert to allow God to show him what he was meant to do and discover that for which he was created.

Our congregations are filled with people on a pilgrimage to a sense
of self-worth and the discovery of a meaningful life. They look for these
things in success, materialism, therapy, service to church and community, relationships, and so forth. Some of those things help, but ultimately
they all fail to bring any lasting sense of wholeness or completeness. Because they are temporal, their impact is fleeting. Only God is eternal and
only God can satisfy fully. Congregations that nurture the prayer life of
members and help them grow in their intimacy with God give them the
opportunity to stand before God, who alone can satisfy their deepest
longing and quench their deepest thirst.

Discovering Your Place in the Body of Christ

Now concerning spiritual gifts, brothers and sisters, I do not want
you to be uninformed.... Now there are varieties of gifts, but the
same spirit;... To each is given the manifestation of the spirit for the
common good.... For just as the body is one and has many members,
and all the members of the body, though many, are one body, so it is
with Christ.... Now you are the body of Christ and individually
members of it.

(1 Corinthians 12:1, 4, 7, 12, 27)

It is one thing to discern your gifts. It is another to discover how to
use them and where they belong in the larger scheme of things both in
the church and in the world. Increasingly, men and women are changing
careers in their thirties and forties. Young people fresh from college are
finding it difficult to get their careers started. Many well-educated and
successful people have confided to me, "I just don't know where I fit in."
Sometimes it is because they do not know or appreciate their gifts. Sometimes they do not know how to use them. Sometimes they have too many
people telling them what to do.

While I was writing this book, I made an extended retreat at Bolton
Abbey, a Cistercian monastery in Ireland. The abbey runs a dairy. In
order to help the monks gather the cows for milking, they purchased a
specially bred and trained dog. The dog's name is Jack. Jack no longer
herds cattle. Instead, he is simply the monastery pet. When I asked why,
I was told, "We ruined him. Jack had too many masters. Each person
gave him different commands. Now all he does is chase the cows."

We all understand Jack's dilemma. We have all kinds of people telling us how to live, helping us decide what to do, and admonishing us about our behavior. In a sense we have too many masters. We are handed scripts and told, "Here is your part. Live it out." Parents have certain demands of children. Children have their own expectations of parents. Spouses expect things from each others. The same is true of employers, coworkers, neighbors, the church, journalists, television commentators, teachers, and the like. We also have our own image of who we think we should be. Consequently, we expend a great deal of energy trying to live up to all those expectations. The more we try, the less like ourselves we become. We become distanced from our true self and live out someone else's image of who we should be. No wonder people cannot find their places in the church or the world.

We forget that it is God who gives these gifts. And it is God who knows best how they should be used. We will struggle to ascertain our unique places in the body until we sit quietly long enough to hear God's gentle breath whisper in our hearts. A composer once said when asked how he found inspiration for his music, "Sometimes if I sit still long enough and listen well enough, I become the instrument for writing down what it is that wants to be said."[3] So it is with discerning our place in the body. God will tell us in God's own time when in prayer we listen and give God the opportunity to speak.

Such are some of the fruits of prayer for the individual. Congregations can have a major role in providing opportunities for members to grow in their understanding of their gifts and how to use them. Helping people grow in their prayer lives might be one of the greatest ministries we can have.

Growth in Sanctity

I asked a saintly octogenarian whether he had grown in holiness, or had he always been so loving. "Oh, my goodness," he blurted in embarrassment, "I have hardly grown at all." Such is his humility.

People who had known him for decades witnessed the remarkable maturing of a Christian in holiness and love, however, so I pressed him further. "You must have grown some."

"Well, if I have, it was God's own doing," he replied.

Protestant churches are good at reminding parishioners about "justification by grace through faith." Sometimes, however, we fail to follow it
with discussions about growth in sanctity.

> You were taught to put away, your former ways of life, your old self,
> which gets corrupted by following illusory desires. Your mind must
> be renewed by a spiritual revolution so that you can put on the new
> self that has been created in God's likeness in true righteousness and
> holiness.
>
> (Ephesians 4:22-24 JB)

Paul so emphasizes this theme of the new self, the new being, or the new
creation that he says nothing else matters, "but a new creation is everything" (Galatians 6:15).

We cannot, however, recreate ourselves. Neither can we by our own
will make ourselves grow in holiness. We do have some control over
behavior, but what goes on inside is God's own domain. We have little
power to change our hearts. All we can do is offer them to God and in
prayer give God the time, space, and opportunity to work in us.

Irenaeus said, "If God is the potter and we are the clay, then let the
clay be moist."[4] He goes on to say that God needs a malleable heart with
which to work. God can soften our hearts through our devotions. We
must, however, keep them moldable.

St. Paul, who speaks from the experience of being "renewed by a
spiritual revolution," wrote, "the fruit of the Spirit is love, joy, peace,
patience, kindness, generosity, faithfulness, gentleness, and self-control.
If we live by the Spirit, let us also be guided by the Spirit" (Galatians
5:22, 25). In the final analysis, to be a Christian is to seek to do God's
will. Ultimately, prayer does not change God; prayer changes the one
who prays and asks to be aligned with God's will.

To See God

From September 1969 until his death in April 1970, a man named Ed
Goetz was one of my intern supervisors. All that fall, Ed—or Dr. Goetz,
as I called him—showed me the pastoral ropes. He also spoke at length
about prayer and devotions. His favorite biblical text was, "My grace is

sufficient for you" (2 Corinthians 12:9). Some of what he told me sunk in; some did not—that is, until early 1970 when Ed's cancer recurred. The outlook was bleak, but Ed did not change much. He still laughed and enjoyed life. He still loved and cherished time with his wife, Dorothy. He still had time to instruct me in the art of living and dying in the faith.

I asked once, "Don't you ever get sad? Don't you ever get angry?"

He replied, "Yes, of course. And I weep sometimes. But God's grace is sufficient for me."

I watched him die slowly over months. God's grace was sufficient. He died filled with anticipation of the resurrection.

Before he became ill, he told me that one of the fruits of a Christian life of prayer is "the ability to see God more easily—to see God in the morning sun and in the midst of suffering and death. It is being able to see the Christ in others and the Christ in yourself. It is to know that God's grace is sufficient to go with us wherever the journey takes us."

We all long to see God and know God intimately. Maybe the greatest gift a lifetime of prayer gives the individual is the ability to see God more easily and in more places. It does not mean there is no struggle. It does mean that people of prayer are equipped with more than their own strength of will. God's grace is indeed sufficient. The gift of prayer is to know it and be grasped by it—and to be sustained by that same grace.

NOTES

Introduction

1. Jacob Needleman, *Lost Christianity* (San Francisco: Harper & Row Publishers, 1985), 20.

Chapter 2

1. Martin Luther's explanation of the Third Article of the Creed, *A Contemporary Translation of Luther's Small Catechism Study Edition*, trans. Timothy J. Wengert (Minneapolis: Augsburg Fortress, 1994), 29.

2. Parker, Percy Livingstone, *The Journal of John Wesley* (Chicago: Moody Press), 64.

3. Martin Luther, "A Simple Way to Pray," Helmut T. Lehmann, ed., *Luther's Works*, vol. 43 (Philadelphia: Fortress Press, 1968), 187ff.

4. Ibid., 193

5. Ibid., 198

6. John W. Doberstein, *Minister's Prayer Book* (Philadelphia: Muhlenberg Press, n.d.), 444.

7. Luther, "A Simple Way to Pray," 193.

Chapter 3

1. Martin Luther, "A Simple Way to Pray," 198.

Chapter 4

1. Jaraslov Pelikan, *The Christian Tradition: A History of the Development of Doctrine*, vol. 1 (Chicago: University of Chicago Press, 1971), 1.

Chapter 6

1. Dietrich Bonhoeffer, *Life Together* (New York: Harper & Row, 1954), 77.

Chapter 8

1. For more information, call or write: Gloria Dei! Lutheran Church, 461 College Parkway, Arnold, MD 21012. (410) 544-3799.

Chapter 9

1. Richard Wright in a lecture in 1968.
2. Karl Menninger, *Whatever Became of Sin* (New York: Hawthorn Books, Inc. 1974), 201.

Chapter 10

1. St. Augustine, *Confessions* (New York: Liveright Publishing Corp., n.d.), 1.
2. Thomas Merton, *Love and Living* (New York: Harcourt Brace, 1979), 40.
3. Mother Teresa of Calcutta, *The Love of Christ: Spiritual Counsels* (New York: Harper and Row, 1982), 7.

Chapter 13

1. The Shalem Institute, 5430 Grosvenor Lane, Bethesda, MD 20814. Shalem has several programs in spiritual direction that you might find extremely beneficial.

2. Thomas Merton, *Thoughts in Solitude* (New York: Farrar, Straus and Giroux, 1982), 18.

Chapter 15

1. Verna Dozier with Celia Hahn, *The Authority of the Laity* (Washington, DC: The Alban Institute, 1982), 40 and 42.

2. Matthew Fox, ed., *Breakthrough: Meister Eckhart's Creation Spirituality in New Translation* (Garden City, NY: Image Books, 1980), 293-324.

Chapter 16

1. Thomas Merton, *Seeds of Contemplation* (New York: New Directions, 1949), 26.

2. I do not recall where I heard this story or who told it.

3. Paul Stookey in concert.

4. St. Iranaeus, *Against Heresies, in The Ante Nicene Fathers*, vol. 1 (Grand Rapids, MI: Eerdmans Publishing Co., 1950), 427.